About the Author

John L. Daly, MBA, CPA, CMA, CPIM is president of Executive Education, Inc. in Chelsea, Michigan. He spent five years in public practice with two large CPA firms followed by fifteen years as chief financial officer for several different manufacturing companies. He has taught continuing professional education for corporate financial professionals since 1995. John has also written many seminars, articles, webinars and another book, *Pricing for Profitability*, published by John C. Wiley & Sons.

Cover by Kerrie Robertson Illustration

First Published in the United States in 2020.

You may contact the author at Daly@ExecutiveEducationInc.com. Please let us know if you find any typos or factual inaccuracies.

www.ExecutiveEducationInc.com

20-12

TOOL & DIE

Love, life and death in a
manufacturing company

A novel by
John L. Daly

Dedication

To my wife, partner and confidant, Nancy J. Daly, and these co-workers and friends:

Jeannie Ballew
Terry Baulch
Bill Belisle
Larry Byrne
Michael Chapman
Dan Chenoweth
Craig Carrell
Bryan Cody
Fred Feiler
Gary Grigowski
Richard Karwic

Hermann Kress
John Levy
Don Minges
Sherri Montoye
Bill O'Brien
Chuck Newman
Barbara Sullivan
Dave Wacnik
Kylie Welling
Diane White

Chapters

Preface

Over my years in the business world, I served as Chief Financial Officer or Chief Operating Officer for six manufacturing companies ranging in size from 100 to 5000 employees. This story combines all six experiences and does not depict any one company or the events occurring therein. The characters represent "types" I have known and do not depict any actual persons except for some of my friends at The Players. I have worked with many excellent managers and have made many lifelong friends in my working life.

We can all learn from the examples of others, both good and bad. I hope that those who read this book are motivated to lead lives that are honest, collaborative and empathetic.

Fairlane Tool and Manuf. Co.
Organizational Chart
As of June 1989

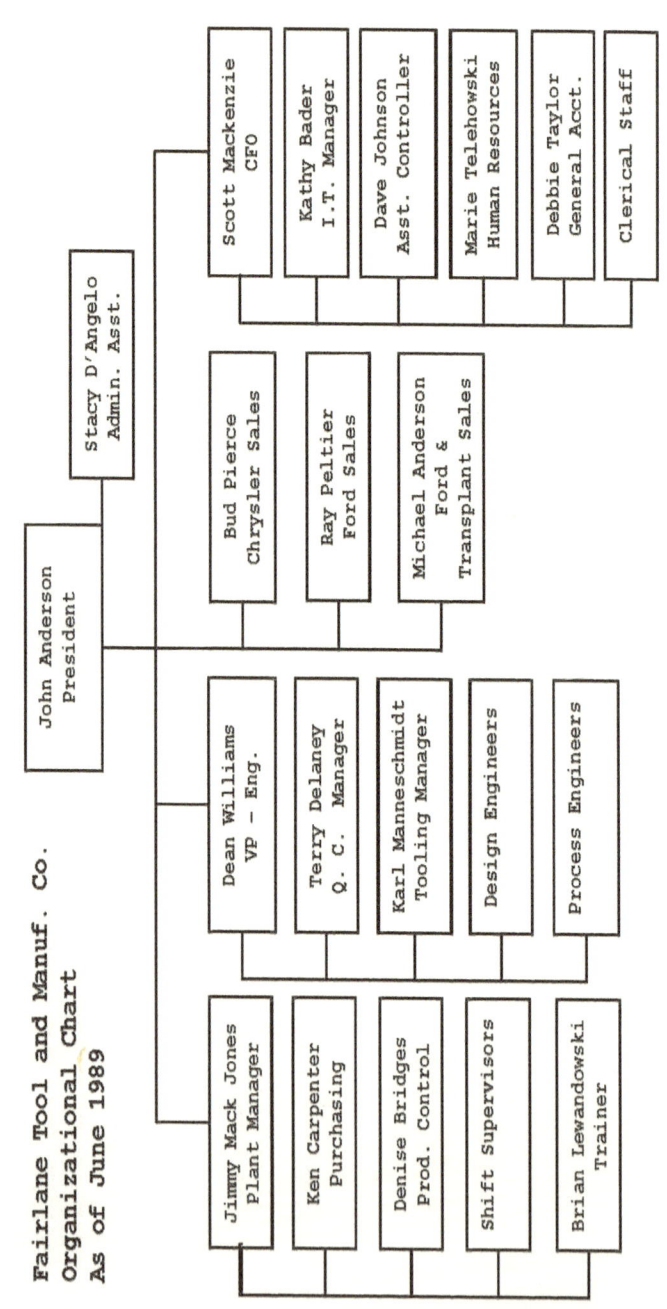

John Anderson — President

Stacy D'Angelo — Admin. Asst.

Scott Mackenzie — CFO
- Kathy Bader — I.T. Manager
- Dave Johnson — Asst. Controller
- Marie Telehowski — Human Resources
- Debbie Taylor — General Acct.
- Clerical Staff

Bud Pierce — Chrysler Sales
Ray Peltier — Ford Sales
Michael Anderson — Ford & Transplant Sales

Dean Williams — VP – Eng.
- Terry Delaney — Q. C. Manager
- Karl Manneschmidt — Tooling Manager
- Design Engineers
- Process Engineers

Jimmy Mack Jones — Plant Manager
- Ken Carpenter — Purchasing
- Denise Bridges — Prod. Control
- Shift Supervisors
- Brian Lewandowski — Trainer

Chapter 1

Fairlane Tool & Manufacturing Co.

In 1989, when this story begins, Metropolitan Detroit is the world's automotive capital, covering most of three Southeast Michigan counties totaling well over 1,000 square miles. The region holds the "Big Three" automakers' headquarters as well as hundreds of auto parts suppliers, large and small.

General Motors headquarters is in the "New Center," a business district on Woodward Avenue, three and a half miles north of downtown Detroit. City offices occupy a cramped building overlooking the Detroit River with a view of Windsor, Ontario a half mile to the South. It is the only place a major Canadian city is south of the U.S. border.

Chrysler's new headquarters and technology center sits at the northern edge of the urban sprawl in Auburn Hills, across I-75 from the Pontiac Silverdome, home of the Detroit Lions. Pontiac was an Ottawa war chief who struggled against British military occupation of the Great Lakes Region, laying siege to Detroit in 1763. The founders named the city after Chief Pontiac and General Motors named its Pontiac Motor Division after the city where it had major automotive assembly operations. Thus, without spending a dime, General Motors benefited from the happy fact that the name Pontiac received frequent mention anytime the Lions played a televised home game. Since William Clay Ford, Henry Ford's grandson, owned the football team, he probably was not fond of the stadium's name.

The city of Dearborn, home of Ford Motor Company, straddles Michigan Avenue nine miles west of downtown Detroit. Ford headquarters has stood near the corner of Michigan Avenue and the Southfield Freeway since 1956, not far from where Henry Ford was born. Ford's estate, Fair Lane is also close by. The names Ford or Fairlane seem to be on everything in Dearborn. The Henry Ford Museum and Greenfield Village, now known collectively as The Henry Ford, is the nation's largest indoor/outdoor museum featuring an amazing collection of historic buildings including Edison's Laboratory, the Wright Brothers' Bicycle shop and dozens more. There is Henry Ford Community College, Edsel Ford High School and the Fairlane Town Center featuring Fairlane Mall. The area also includes Ford's Product Development Center, test track, dozens of other Ford buildings, and many of their suppliers providing tens of thousands of jobs.

Of ten random people, three will love their job, one will hate their job and the remaining six exist somewhere in the middle. Some companies are easier to love than others. In great companies, everyone works as a team, holding each other accountable in an environment that provides the freedom to make decisions, succeed and grow.

An organization's culture is fragile. Management must nurture the relationships with its customers, vendors, and employees for years to build a great company. However, one simple error of sufficient magnitude can destroy it all, turning love into hate, fear, and a feeling of betrayal in just a few short days.

Fairlane Tool and Manufacturing Company was a great company for seven years.

Chapter 2

The Challenge

Wednesday, April 19, 1989

"Where do you want this?" Michael Anderson walked into the Dearborn Hyatt Regency Hotel meeting room carrying a transparency projector. Scott Mackenzie, Fairlane Tool and Manufacturing's young Vice President - Finance was already in the room talking to the server who would handle the company's quarterly management meeting.

"Let's put it over on the sideboard until we need it."

In many companies, conflicts between accounting and sales are legendary. Sales complains the margins accounting wants are too high and accounting keeps a close watch over sales to prevent them from selling too cheaply or spending too much. Sales people often think of accounting as "The Sales Prevention Department."

Fairlane Tool was not like that. At 27-years-old, Michael Anderson had never worked with another chief financial officer, but he knew that Bud Pierce and Ray Peltier, the sales department's two gray-haired veterans, thought highly of Mackenzie, who at thirty-six, was more than two decades their junior.

In this context, it made sense that Fairlane's CFO and the company's youngest salesperson would work well together and be good friends.

The agenda for the company's quarterly management meeting was always the same – cocktails at 5:30, dinner at 6:15 and business at 7 pm. Tonight, Michael would present at the meeting for the first time.

Precisely at 7:00, Michael followed CEO John Anderson's opening remarks.

Michael quoted Ford's internal policy memo almost verbatim. "In three years, we will not deal with any suppliers with less than $100 million in sales except for certain niche suppliers whose products are essential to the fit, finish and functionality of our vehicles."

Michael had obtained the memo from one of Ford's purchasing managers. Ford represented just over 70% of Fairlane's sales.

The news startled Don Kelley, the company's Livonia plant manager, and the half of the management team members who were not already privy to the news. "We're not even a third of that now. I hope we're one of the exceptions."

"Yes, we're safe for now," John responded, "but that doesn't mean we're safe for the long term. We've got to grow to stay in the game. Scott has the numbers. Let's look at what we're up against."

Scott moved from his seat at the middle of the long table to the end opposite John in front of the projection screen. Michael put the transparency projector on the table's end and plugged it into the wall. A moment later, Scott placed a transparency on the glass surface showing a graph.

"Here's where we've come in the last five years. We were at barely nine million in 1984 and I project we'll be at just under thirty for the year ending in July for a really strong twenty-seven percent annual growth rate."

Scott paused and looked around the room for comprehension. He saw most of the heads nodding in agreement and continued.

"Based on what these guys have sold for the next three years," he said, gesturing at the side of the table where Michael, Bud and Ray sat together, "that growth rate really accelerates."

"That sounds good," Ken observed.

"It also sounds really scary," said Karl. "That much verk must be a couple hundred new tools."

"Where are we going to get the press capacity?" Jimmy asked.

"What kind of assembly equipment are we talking about?" asked Don.

Scott responded, "Now you're beginning to see the problems, and I'll add one more. Investing in equipment, training and everything else we'll need is going to require a lot of cash that we don't have. So far, our bank has lent us eighty percent of the money we need for new equipment, but even coming up with the remaining twenty percent is going to be a challenge for us at this growth rate."

"Does the stock option plan help us with this?" Dean Williams asked.

"It does," Scott responded. "Everybody at this table has options to buy 2% of the company. Comerica will finance 80% of your purchase, so any money you invest is extra equity and helps us borrow more. If we can get these new jobs into production, the stock will be a really good investment."

Ray quipped, "And if we can't make it happen, the stock certificate is suitable for framing and will look good on your wall."

Nervous laughter broke out and the team spent the rest of the meeting walking through the details of Fairlane's three-year plan.

Chapter 3

Marie Telehowski

Friday, May 12, 1989

Sliding into her blue Ford Taurus station wagon in a visitor parking space outside Fairlane Tool and Manufacturing Company, Marie Telehowski locked her seat belt in place. Now, at age 42, she was going to start a career.

Marie felt simultaneously exhilarated and frightened. Her only so-called "real job" in seventeen years was working at the Southland Mall J.L. Hudson's department store at Christmastime for three years before going back to get her BBA degree at the University of Michigan - Dearborn. Returning to school had been a big life change, but up until now, it seemed like she had really been a stay-at-home mom with a time-consuming hobby.

She wondered how Jack would handle the change. Her job offer was $5,000 more than he earned. Somehow, she feared the combination of her job and making that much more money would be too big a blow to his masculinity at one time. She knew several women her age at business school whose marriages didn't even last until graduation.

"I'll tell him the offer is less and hide the rest," she thought. "I pay the bills and do the taxes. He'll never know. As for his masculinity, I know how to pump that up."

Marie started the car and 5:05 PM appeared on her dashboard. Fairlane was at most ten minutes from their suburban home in Taylor. Jack's office on Outer Drive was a bit further. He frequently arrived home at 5:20 if he left Ford at precisely 5 PM. Her plan to break the news the way she wanted depended on her getting home first.

The job seemed like an almost perfect fit. Only four miles from home and everyone seemed so nice! Fitting in worried her the most. Everyone seemed so young. Scott Mackenzie, her new boss, was only 36 years old and everyone else in the administrative area looked younger. Some of the clerks looked young enough to be her daughter. During her tour, she saw several men with gray hair, few women and she guessed that at least half of the company was in their 20s.

During the second interview, she was able to talk to two other women. Kathy Bader, the information technology manager, was impressive. Though they had only a half-hour together, Marie had already concluded that Kathy was one of the smartest and most articulate women she had ever met. On top of it, her slim figure, rich brown hair and almond-shaped brown eyes gave her a somewhat exotic look.

Marie had an opportunity to ask Kathy about something that seemed very strange in her first interview. Instead of seating her across from his desk, Mackenzie sat her next to the desk, as if she were a visiting colleague, rather than a potential employee. It seemed that he was recruiting as much as interviewing her. She felt like he was treating her as an equal. When she tried to call him "Mr. Mackenzie" at the end of the first interview, he told her that everyone was on a first name basis at Fairlane and she should call him "Scott". That made her a lot more comfortable. However, she wondered about it.

Kathy confirmed that everybody called each other by their first name at Fairlane and being a woman wasn't going to be a handicap, at least not in the department Scott managed.

"Both his mother and grandmother worked," Kathy explained. "He probably wasn't allowed to develop any sexist attitudes at home."

Debbie Taylor, the senior accounting clerk, provided the same opinion, saying, "He's the real deal."

Kathy and Debbie had very different backgrounds. Both were smart, assertive, thin and fit, but the resemblance ended there. Kathy was polished and Debbie wasn't. Kathy was obviously well educated, fashionably dressed and from an upper middle-class professional background, whereas Debbie had a high school diploma, dressed inexpensively and had an unpolished vocabulary.

Marie was relieved to see that Jack was not home as their garage's double door opened. All the lights were off, and the house was dark except for the daylight coming through the kitchen window and the closed vertical blinds covering the living room sliding glass door.

Stepping out of her black heels, she confirmed from the family calendar that their two sons would not be home from sports practice for almost an hour. She took the combination kitchen chair / step stool, found a bottle of red wine in the cabinet over the sink and found two wine glasses on another cabinet's top shelf. Just as she uncorked the bottle, she heard the garage door lurch into action.

"I wish I had more time," she thought as she quickly poured wine into both glasses, pouring considerably more into his. She took two quick gulps and posed facing the mudroom door to await Jack's entrance.

Marie met him still dressed in the red blazer, white blouse and navy-blue skirt she wore for her interview. She reached for his tie and pulled his face down to hers. His 6'2" frame compared to her 5'3" height, required him to bend at the knees. The kiss was long, deep and purposeful. "I take it you got the job," he remarked.

She handed him the full wineglass and said, "Joey is playing soccer and Steve has baseball practice until 6:00. The new Human Resources Manager of Fairlane Tool & Manufacturing would like to debrief you in her chambers."

Still holding his tie, Marie led him from the kitchen through the dining room down the hallway to their bedroom, letting go of his tie as she closed and locked the bedroom door. He set his wine glass on the bedside table and reached to undo his tie.

"Did I tell you to undress?" she asked, pushing him to a seated position on the bed. She removed his tie and penny loafers and then swung his legs onto their Queen-sized bed. "I'm going to take care of everything this evening."

"I could get used to this," Jack said as she disappeared into their walk-in closet. Marie removed her red jacket, the skirt and panty hose. As she began to unbutton her blouse, her eyes met his in the dresser mirror. She gave him a "bad boy" look and closed the closet door so she could keep at least part of her preparation a surprise.

She soon stood nude in their closet except for the new, white-lace bra she wore to the interview. What should she wear? Some clothes could add excitement, but since her goal was to have sex with her husband as soon as possible, much more than a bra would be overdoing it. Jack had always been preoccupied with her tits. Frankly, every guy she ever dated had been preoccupied with them although she didn't let a guy actually see them until her senior prom. It was her Catholic upbringing. Half of her high school classmates were on third base by their sophomore year, but she didn't let a guy see her breasts until their fourth date to the senior prom. That guy dropped her five dates later after another girl screwed him at a beach party Marie couldn't attend.

Marie began dating Jack two months later. Jack seemed to be willing to let their relationship advance in slow increments, and when she finally let him have sex with her 18 months later, she was reasonably certain they were in a long-term relationship.

Marie emerged from the closet wearing only a black bra and the white interview blouse with all the buttons undone. She stood briefly at the foot of the bed, silhouetted in the dark room by the light coming through the blinds covering the large bedroom window. Seeing his big smile, she climbed onto the queen-sized bed, straddling him on her knees. She leaned over to put her glasses on the headboard, intentionally positioning her right breast temptingly near his mouth.

Marie said, "Where were we? Oh, yes, your debriefing," as she reached for his belt.

Forty minutes later, the slamming back door awakened them.

"Mom, Dad, we're home!" came their younger son Joey's voice.

Jack called out; "We're changing" jumped out of bed and hurriedly pulled on a casual shirt with his slacks.

Marie, still groggy, rushed to the closet for some clothes as Jack sat on the bed to put on his socks. The black bra and white blouse now carelessly resided on the floor next to the bed. Jack slipped out the door to hear Joey exclaim, "We won 5-2 and Steve gets to start tomorrow!" Their older son looked around the kitchen and sniffed the air. He asked. "Hey, where's Mom and why isn't dinner cooking?"

Jack replied, "Mom had a late interview and got the job. She'll tell us all about it at dinner. We're going out to eat."

Marie emerged from the bedroom moments later barefoot, in blue jeans and a red polo shirt. "Pizza?" She said.

Chapter 4

Dave Johnson

May 19, 1989

Thump, thump, thump, thump, thump....

The afternoon was unseasonably warm for the third Friday in May. The big truck bay doors were open on both the north and the south ends of Fairlane Tool & Manufacturing's large white sheet metal building.

From the parking lot, Dave Johnson could hear the dull rhythm of the stamping presses through the open doors as he sat in his five-year old Ford Taurus sedan with driver's side door open and all the windows down.

Dave's air conditioning quit the previous September but, being only three years out of business school and not flush with cash, he decided to wait until spring to get it fixed. Monday's temperatures in Grand Rapids were only in the 50's, but now he was in Dearborn, sitting in a black car in a treeless asphalt parking lot in 85-degree heat.

He looked at his watch - Twelve fifty-five. His interview would start in five minutes and yet he was sweating profusely. His brown pinstriped suit jacket lay on the car's back seat. He would have little time to deal with his perspiration, loose tie and the rolled-up cuffs of his long-sleeve business shirt.

He pulled napkins from a Burger King bag and threw the bag on the back floor. Drying the perspiration from his face and neck, he rebuttoned his collar and straightened his tie, using the rearview mirror to check the knot alignment. *I don't look cool and calm*, he thought, seeing his face was more than a little flushed.

Johnson's face was distinctly average looking. He stood five foot eleven with medium brown hair, hazel eyes and had an otherwise unremarkable physique. In either profile, he actually verged on handsome, but the lack of symmetry between the left and right sides of his face gave him a slightly odd look.

Rolling up the windows, Dave stepped out of the car and pressed the unlock button to access the back door. With both doors open, he buttoned his cuffs and put on the suit jacket. Taking the brown leather portfolio containing his résumé, he hit "lock," closed both doors, and walked toward the company's entrance trying not to look nervous.

The first glass door opened into a vestibule noticeably cooler than the outside air. Beyond the second glass door, Dave found the lobby positively freezing. A very plain, but competent-looking young woman with wire-rimmed glasses and long, frizzy light-brown hair opened the sliding receptionist window on the right wall before he could reach it and asked how she could help. "I'm here to see Scott Mackenzie," he told her. She nodded and lifted a finger to indicate "one moment" as she picked up the ringing phone on the operator console.

Dave looked around the lobby as the receptionist took the call. The displays were familiar from his first visit. The wall opposite the receptionist's window featured a gallery of quality awards from customers Ford and Chrysler. On the wall opposite the entry door, was an architect's rendition of the building, dated 1987. The new building provided an obvious source of pride to Fairlane team members. Less than two years before, the company occupied a manufacturing plant less than half the size of this 85,000 square foot facility.

Thump, Thump, Thump, Thump. The press sounds seemed more distant from where Dave stood in the lobby, though he knew he must now be some fifty feet closer. The sound seemed low and muffled and he had the vague notion he felt the vibrations through his feet on the gray ceramic-tiled floor.

Does this count as the second interview or the third? Dave wondered. He knew companies usually made job offers at the end of a third interview, but he did not know if the initial phone interview counted. Since he currently lived nearly a three-hour drive from Dearborn, Scott Mackenzie, Fairlane's Chief Financial Officer, talked with him for nearly an hour and a half in his first phone call. The call felt like an interview, even though they did not talk face to face.

Dave thought about what he saw during his first visit two weeks earlier. The two doors on the North side of the large building allowed covered flatbed semis carrying coil steel to back inside the building, unloading without exposure to rain or snow. Fairlane stored the coiled steel only a few feet away from those doors. As needed, forklift drivers moved skids of steel coils southward to the big progressive die stamping presses. These presses turned the steel into stamped parts. Some parts required only one operation while others went through secondary stamping operations, plating at an outside processor or assembly at Fairlane's Plymouth Road Assembly plant in Livonia, a few miles to the northwest. Dave calculated that the closest press sat about 100 feet away since he was standing in the lobby at the center of the building's east side.

"He'll be right with you," the receptionist said. "Thank you, Joan," Dave responded, noting the nameplate reading

"Joan Robbins – Communications Specialist" next to the window.

Turning around and feigning interest in the wall displays, he felt his face and forehead for any sign of residual sweat. Thankfully, the cold lobby had stopped his perspiration. Then, Scott Mackenzie opened the lobby door.

Mackenzie, the Vice President – Finance, did not look like an accountant. At five-foot seven he was a good four inches shorter than Johnson, with strawberry blond hair, wire rim glasses and freckles. He wore a long-sleeved blue and white shirt with cuffs rolled up to the elbows, and a loosened striped tie sat slightly off-center of his unbuttoned collar. Mackenzie wore navy suit pants and slightly scuffed black wing tip shoes. He obviously shed his suit jacket hours ago. Johnson remembered Mackenzie's exceptionally broad shoulders and muscular looking forearms covered with the same strawberry blonde hair. Mackenzie had a direct, manly air with a strong handshake despite having noticeably smaller hands than Dave's. He had a cheerful and energetic demeanor.

"The plan," he said, getting right to the point, "is for you to meet some of our other team members. Last time you heard me tell about what a great place this is to work, but I thought you might like a few other opinions. I've got you scheduled to meet with Ken Carpenter, the purchasing manager; Debbie Taylor, our senior accounting clerk; Kathy Bader, the IT manager and if we can work it in, John Anderson, the president. Come on, I'll introduce you to Ken."

The lobby door opened to the central hallway running north to south through Fairlane's offices. They turned left toward the building's south end walking by the open door of an empty conference room before passing through another door to an area with three offices. Dave saw a black and white plastic nameplate that read "Ken Carpenter – Purchasing Manager" outside the door as Mackenzie led him into the last office.

A friendly middle aged-looking guy rose as Scott and Dave entered the office. With slightly thinning light brown hair and a good start on a beer gut, Ken Carpenter stood, perhaps an inch shorter than Mackenzie at about 5'6". He wore a short-sleeved dark blue shirt, an inexpensive looking striped tie, khaki slacks and casual brown shoes.

Before leaving, Scott and Ken talked about a vendor matter giving Dave some time to glance around the room. Besides the buying guides and product samples normally found in a purchasing manager's office, Dave noted hockey paraphernalia everywhere. A framed Detroit Red Wings poster signed by Steve Yzerman hung on one wall. On top of a file cabinet rested a Red Wings hat as well as a hockey puck serving as a paperweight. A summer-weight Wings jacket hung on a hook and another wall displayed three team pictures showing Carpenter with a youth hockey team labeled "Whalers" dated 1987, 1988 and 1989. The boys in the third picture appeared to be about nine. In another picture, an adolescent girl in a figure skating outfit stood next to a boy in the same Whaler's uniform. *Ok*, Dave thought, *he has an eleven-year old daughter and a nine-year-old son.* That would put Ken in his early to mid-30s.

As Mackenzie left, Dave turned his attention from the Yzerman jersey back to Ken. "Are you a fan?" Ken asked.

"Sort of," Dave replied. "I mean, I don't really know much about hockey, but it looks like a fun sport." Dave asked a question about the pictures of Ken's kids and soon learned a lot about them both, including that Ken's daughter could out skate any boy on the hockey team forward or backward.

Soon, Ken refocused the conversation to the first order of business on his mind. "Look, I just had a burger with grilled onions and a side order of onion rings for lunch. I need a Coke to try to get the taste out of my mouth. Why don't we wander over to the break room and I'll buy you something to drink? You'll need these," Ken said as he handed Dave a pair of safety glasses.

Dave had been unaware of the distant thumping since his wait in the lobby. Indeed, he didn't notice the thumping as they walked from Ken's office in the building's southeast corner northward through the central office hallway. He did not notice it as they walked through the fire door into the office break area, even though they walked closer and closer to the thumping's source. As they opened the first of two doors in a hallway between the office break area and the plant, the thumping sound became very loud, very abruptly and then even louder as Ken opened the second door. Thirty feet to the right as they entered the plant were the big open bay doors through which Dave had heard thumping in the parking lot. Fifty feet to the left was a 300-ton Minster press cranking out auto parts in a dull rhythm.

"Fifty strokes a minute," Dave remembered Mackenzie saying on the tour during his previous visit.

"We call the presses in this area "automatics" because they continuously cycle when they're running. Automatic presses run progressive dies, which means the tooling inside the press has multiple stations and the machine's feeder equipment advances the steel through the stations progressively; that is, first one station, then the next."

Mackenzie displayed an impressive knowledge of the company's manufacturing operations. His lesson on stamping presses transitioned into a lesson on stamping dies.

"Dies consist of upper and lower halves. We attach the upper half to the ram, which is the part of the press you see moving up and down in the open press window in the middle. The bottom part of the window, which doesn't move, is the bolster. The first station may punch a hole or cut away a little bit of metal, the second station may cut away more metal and later some bending or forming may happen, then the final die station cuts the part away from the coil."

Taking Dave to one end of the press, Mackenzie had pointed to parts detaching into two different steel skids.

"Most progressive dies are "two-out," meaning they make either two identical or two mirror image parts per stroke. Besides being more efficient, making two parts at the same time puts a uniform force on each side of the coil as it passes through the die, discouraging the steel from pulling to one side of the die or the other. In theory, these presses could make 6000 parts per hour, but because of coil changes, and other issues, getting even 3000 parts per hour is pretty good."

Later, a question occurred to Dave about the manufacturing process. Since he had not asked Mackenzie the question, he decided to ask the purchasing manager. "Ken, what is the difference between a tool and a die?"

"Good question" Ken said. "And I would be hard pressed to give you a clear answer. I think a tool is any specialized equipment used to make something. The term die is probably more specific. But, frankly, I'm not sure. When some people see the name Fairlane *Tool* and

Manufacturing Company, they assume we're a tool and die shop. We have always made tooling, but our primary business has always been stamping. As you've probably figured out, tooling is probably less than five percent of our sales."

Ken fed a dollar into the vending machine and invited Dave to make a selection. He chose a Diet Coke and Ken chose a Coke Classic from the same machine. Dave couldn't help but see the irony that Ken needed the diet soft drink a lot more than he did.

"So, where are you from?" Ken asked as they walked back to the other end of the office area.

"Goshen, Indiana, originally," Dave replied. I went to Ball State then took a job with BDO Seidman in Grand Rapids. My girlfriend started work for a Detroit accounting firm, so I'm looking for a job here."

Ken Carpenter, Dave learned, was one of the management team's longest standing members. He grew up in Canton, Michigan a western Detroit suburb in the days when Canton was just a rural township filled with farms, a couple of crossroads bars and filling stations. Ken put himself through Oakland University in the northern suburbs on the seven-year plan working at Fairlane as a part-time job. Somewhere in the process, he married a girl he dated in high school, moved to Plymouth, and lived with their two children less than five miles from their parents.

"How big was the company when you started?" Dave asked.

"Pretty darned small," Ken replied. "I don't know how much of the story Scott told you, but the company is only fifteen years old. John Anderson became a sales rep after he retired from the Lions…"

"The Detroit Lions?" Dave interrupted.

"Yes. He played tight end. Got drafted out of the University of Michigan and spent about seven years in the pros. He started a few years, was all-pro once but had some chronic knee problems and eventually gave it up. He worked for some other ex-Lion's sales rep agency for a couple of years, bought a minority interest in one of his clients. When the client filed for Chapter 11, John figured he could manage a stamping company better than they had, bought some of their old equipment, hired some of their people and kept enough of their old customers to start the company."

Today, "Terry Delaney, Karl Manneschmidt and a couple of the production workers are the only Silent Tool people left. Terry oversees quality control and Karl manages the tool room. Both of them are top-notch technical guys. Terry studied quality control at Henry Ford but never graduated. Karl is a German master tool & die maker from Frankfurt, Germany. Came over in the mid-70s I think."

Dave nodded and let the purchasing manager continue to talk.

"I started with the company only a few months after that. I ran a spot welder on the night shift. It was dirty work, but the money was good, and I was making enough to pay for gas and tuition. There must have been about 25 people then. We probably have 280 employees now, which is why the company needs another accountant."

The topic ranged from subject to subject after that. After another half hour, Dave was comfortable enough with Ken to ask him the biggest question he had on his mind. "What is Scott Mackenzie like to work with?"

Ken paused for a minute to think about it. "I think that Scott Mackenzie is one of the smartest people I know, certainly the smartest person in the company. He would deny it. In fact, he would probably say that honor belongs to Kathy Bader but I'm not sure she would agree with him. You know how some people are really book smart but can't apply any of it to the real world? Scott isn't like that. He knows the real world, understands manufacturing and is a really down to earth guy. I really like working with him and I think that you would too."

A woman whom Dave judged to be in her early 30s interrupted the conversation. Slim and wearing a short, tight fitting, but business appropriate dress, she had a short, up-turned nose, brown eyes and obviously bleached blonde hair judging from the inch of brown roots where her hair parted in the middle.

"Excuse me for interrupting," she said as she rapped on the already open door.

"We've got a change in schedule. Kathy and Scott are working on some sort of a shipping crisis, and John wants to leave early this afternoon. He can see Mr. Johnson in a few minutes if you're done here."

While Dave was sure that Ken would be willing to talk all afternoon, meeting the company president would be much more important. The woman offered to take him to his office and so he followed her. Halfway down the hall, she stopped as if she had suddenly remembered something, extended her hand and said, "Oh, by the way, I'm Debbie Taylor. I'm on your schedule later this afternoon."

She led him back to the other end of the office area, through the fire door at the north end of accounting and turned right to climb a set of wide stairs to the second-floor offices.   A dark-haired woman squinted at her computer screen in a reception area at the top of the stairs. Dave could see into the president's office through the floor-to-ceiling glass panel next to his office door opposite the stairs. The tall and distinguished looking executive clearly enjoyed talking to whomever sat at the other end of his phone conversation.

Debbie introduced the woman as Stacy D'Angelo and left Dave with her. D'Angelo smiled slightly, offering him a seat. She made a minute of small talk before explaining she needed to get a letter out by the end of the day.

"Kathy gave me a new word processing program a few weeks ago and I still haven't learned how to use it. I liked Pro Write, and I'm not sure why we had to change."

"What are you using now?" Dave asked.

"I think that it's just called *Word*" she responded.   "I don't really like it because it seems a lot more complicated. I wasn't going to switch, but yesterday Kathy removed the old program from my computer saying our license expired. It sounded like just a story to me. How would anyone know if I was using their program?"

Dave considered trying to explain software licensing to her but decided against it and merely expressed sympathy for her plight.

Dave's seat faced the left side of Stacy's desk. He looked straight ahead as Stacy squinted at her computer screen. She had dark features and he concluded that she might have gypsy heritage. She was pretty, although she might have been much prettier with orthodontic care for her several crooked teeth. He judged her to be about 28 years old and there was a wedding ring with a small diamond on her left hand.

"Forget to wear your glasses today?" Dave asked, observing her squinting at the computer screen again.

"I don't like to wear them," she said. "I think they make me look ugly. Anyhow I get along just fine without them most of the time."

"Have you tried contacts?" Dave offered. "I've worn them for years."

"Once, but I just couldn't get used to the concept of putting a piece of glass in my eye. I'm supposed to wear glasses when I'm driving so I keep a set in my car in case I need them. You know, to read signs and things."

Ordinarily, Dave might have expressed his mortification that someone who couldn't see would drive without their glasses, but at that moment, the president opened the door and extended him an outstretched hand.

John Anderson stood about 6'3" with a head of thick graying hair and what seemed to be perfect posture. Dave had no trouble imagining Anderson as an All-Pro tight end.

Upon entering the offices, he could see why Anderson still wore his suit jacket late on an 85-degree Friday afternoon. Unlike the rest of the offices, which were a normal room temperature, Anderson's office was positively freezing like the lobby. "If you don't mind', Anderson said, "I'm going to leave the door open. The air conditioning system in this building has never worked quite right and it will warm up a little in here if we leave the door open."

For a company president's office, the furnishings seemed modest. The office's unusually large size constituted the only sign of extravagance. As in the rest of the offices, off-white paint covered the walls and gray ceramic tiles covered the floor. Dave learned later that Anderson himself had come up with the idea for the tiled floors. Since people routinely wore the same dirty shoes from the stamping plant into the offices, the oils and metal shavings that often become imbedded in the soles of steel-toed shoes would quickly ruin carpet and scar vinyl floor coverings. In that environment, the tile floors were very durable and practical.

Only two clues revealed Anderson ever played football. On one wall was a large, framed photograph of Michigan Stadium. Next to it, mounted in another frame, hung a block "M" varsity letter and certificate.

Anderson offered him a seat at the round table. "Scott seems to think very highly of your accounting skills," Anderson said. "I took a semester of accounting in college, but frankly I didn't do very well. I think I got a "C," so I'm not going to ask you any accounting questions. We're just supposed to get to know each other a little bit and I'm supposed to tell you about the company."

"What was your major?" Dave asked.

"Well," replied Anderson, "I started out in mechanical engineering, but that just wasn't going to be possible playing football. The coaches wanted me to be a communications major, but I chose marketing instead. I wasn't much of a student, but fortunately some of what they tried to teach me stuck."

"Did you play for Bo Schembechler?"

"No, he didn't start at Michigan until 1969. I was there a few years before that. I've gotten to know him since though. Good guy."

Dave saw a copy of his own résumé on Anderson's desk as he came in. It impressed him that the president did not bring it over to the round table as a crib sheet and seemed to know major facts such as where he attended college and where he was working now. Most of the meeting involved Anderson telling Dave about the company.

"Eight years ago, the auto industry was in a real slump. My controller quit and I wasn't sure if our assembly plant in Plymouth was going to work out. Our product line was a bunch of cats and dogs - hinges, brackets and braces, just about anything we could make from a bar or a coil of steel that would go on an automobile. Even though I'm not really an engineer, I found I had a talent for it. I was getting work from Ford by looking at parts other companies made and redesigning them so we could make them cheaper. We had some pretty good growth, but it wasn't particularly organized."

Anderson reached over to a drawer and pulled out two similar looking parts, both about 18 inches long. "This is the before," Anderson said, handing Dave a metal tube whose flattened ends formed a slight "Z" shape. "This is after." Anderson handed Dave a second part. The second brace featured the same flat ends, but the body consisted of flat steel bent into a "V" to give it strength. "Tubing costs more than plain hot rolled steel, so I saved them some money with this design," Anderson said.

"Are these current parts?" Dave asked.

"No, they're from the late 70s to early 80s. I just keep them around to show how far we've come."

Anderson continued, "We put in our first computer in 1981. Dan, the previous controller, worked with the software people to put the system in. Afterward he decided he'd rather be a computer salesman than an accountant and went to work for the software company. We were still small then and for a few months, I did without a controller. Every month Coopers and Lybrand would send someone in for a few days to help close the books. That was in 1982. When the accountants came up with a bunch of big retroactive adjustments one month, I thought maybe we should really have a Controller again but what I really wanted to hire was a computer person. I knew we couldn't afford both. Not wanting to spend a lot of money on headhunters, I contacted the U of M business school alumni office and lucked out by finding a computer guy who was also a CPA and that's how we got Scott Mackenzie."

"Mackenzie is a computer guy?" Dave asked, somewhat surprised by this revelation.

"Yes, his undergraduate degree is in computer science and at Michigan he majored in accounting in their MBA program. I think he mostly worked in computer consulting when he worked at Arthur Andersen." He paused momentarily. "No relation."

Because Anderson was smiling, Dave decided he was making a joke. Obviously, the CEO couldn't think Dave needed an explanation that he was unrelated to the long-deceased founder of the world's largest accounting firm. Arthur Andersen & Company was spelled differently anyhow. Dave smiled at the joke and nodded.

"Anyhow, after a few months Scott came to me with an observation. He said we needed a market niche to survive long term, something we could do better than anybody else in the world. This sounded like what my marketing professors tried to teach me at business school. I thought about it a few days and figured we should specialize in hood hinges.

"So, about that time," Anderson continued, "American automotive companies went to Japan to find out why they were being beaten so badly and brought back many ideas they learned from Japanese companies. Japanese companies organize into what they call a *keiretsu*. You can think of a *keiretsu* as a pyramid-shaped group of interrelated businesses. At the top of the pyramid is a bank, the bank owns large, but minority stock interests in large industrial companies. Some of the bank's managers sit on the industrial company's board, giving them significant influence over the operations although not actual control. The bank, of course, provides financing as part of the relationship. In turn, the large industrial company owns an interest in many of their suppliers and holds seats on the suppliers' boards and may provide some of management as well. These suppliers have similar relationships with even smaller companies until you get down to a tiny company that may make nuts and bolts. The Sumitomo *keiretsu*," Anderson continued, "is an example. Sumitomo Bank, one of the world's largest banks, owns interests in Mazda Motors and Sumitomo Steel. These *keiretsus* allow Japanese companies to be more highly leveraged because the customer relationships involve less risk."

Where did he learn about leverage? Dave wondered. He knew many CEOs had no idea how to even read a balance sheet. He smiled, looked at Anderson intently and nodded.

"A Japanese automaker is likely to use a single supplier for similar parts on all of their vehicles. If you make brake pedal assemblies for Mazda, you are likely to be the only company providing brake pedal assemblies on every vehicle Mazda makes. The company may make no parts at all for the other Japanese car manufacturers because Nissan and Toyota are in different *keiretsus*."

Dave nodded and tried to look like he was listening intently. So far, he thought, the interview was going really well.

"The *keiretsu* was something the American car companies thought was a good idea. While Ford didn't want to invest in their suppliers or put people on their board, it made sense to them to develop suppliers who were experts in the various kinds of parts Ford purchased. Instead of buying from generalist suppliers like we used to be, they would use far fewer suppliers who gained cost efficiencies through specialization and economies of scale."

"Is Mazda Fairlane's only Japanese customer?" Dave asked.

"For now," Anderson responded. "We got into Mazda through our Ford connection since Ford owns thirty-something percent of Mazda. We're not making any Mazda parts yet, but we will next year. Mazda is designing the new Ford Escort and they have the responsibility to choose suppliers. Mazda had the option not to use us, but they did. We think we'll be into Honda in a year or so, but there's nothing definite yet. They've sent teams out to look at us three times now. So far we think they like what they see."

"That's good!" was all the response Dave could manage. He figured he didn't need to say much because Anderson seemed to be in a talking mood. He knew that when the prospective boss wants to talk it means he is in a recruiting mode.

"Actually, that's why I have that area over there," Anderson said pointing to the cluster with the gray sofa and three armchairs. I did a trip to Japan a few years ago and was able to tour eight Japanese companies. Almost everyone I visited had a set-up like this. The president always sits in the middle, but the person on the right does most of the talking. At one company, the president sat through the whole meeting with his head down and his eyes closed. I think he was asleep!"

Anderson got more serious. "The bottom line is that we need to get a lot bigger. Eventually, the big three are likely to stop dealing with small suppliers like us. In the last ten years, they have consolidated from about 1000 suppliers to 300. I wouldn't be surprised if it wasn't 50 within 10 years. They keep making exceptions for certain niche suppliers. We made the cut because of our hinge specialty and, in fact, were named their "commodity team leader" for hood hinges, meaning we will make all the hood hinges that Ford uses. That specialty isn't going to keep us in the game forever, though.

"I anticipate Scott will spend some significant time helping me look at acquisitions in the next few years. We want to find some other niche suppliers whose product lines would be compatible with ours. Those products might include latches, or other mechanical assemblies like fuel filler doors. There is a reason we are trying to hire an assistant controller even though there is no Controller position. We think we'll need a couple of extra financial people over the next few years and we want to provide anyone who joins us an opportunity to grow with us."

Anderson looked at his watch. "Hey, it's been fun to talk with you. My wife and I are trying to get on the road early to get to our lake place before the weekend traffic gets bad. Do you have any questions for me?"

Dave thought it might be bad form to keep the company president from his weekend any longer, so he thanked him for his time. Anderson put him back in Stacy's hands while she tried to figure out whom he should talk with next. Since the phones of both Debbie Taylor and Scott Mackenzie were busy, she reconnected him with Ken Carpenter who collected Dave from the chair in front of Stacy's desk.

Ken took Dave to Scott's open door. He was on the phone, but he waved them in anyhow and they sat in the chairs across from his desk. Ken cradled yet another cold Coke in his hands. Clearly, he was enjoying the break in the action and showed interest in the shipping crisis he knew was going on. Since it was now mid Friday afternoon and many other managers left early, the problem somehow landed on Scott's desk.

As Scott talked, a woman entered the office. Unlike Ken and Dave, she did not hesitate for Scott to recognize her outside the threshold but barged in as if there couldn't possibly be anything more important than what she had to say. She was an attractive brunette whose outfit was particularly attention grabbing. Tucked into her nearly knee-high boots were tight blue pants. Her blouse, if he could call it that, was more like a red and white stripped bustier onto which the designer attached padded shoulders and short sleeves. Holding her straight brown bangs off her forehead was a stars-and-stripes headband that almost seemed like a tiara. While her attire was not immodest, Dave thought the outfit was sexy. In fact, he had the general impression she was wearing a Wonder Woman costume.

Seeing her enter the room, Scott quickly ended his conversation and gave her his full attention.

"As we thought," she said. "We sent an ASN[1] first thing on Monday morning, the carrier picked up the parts

---

[1] An Advanced Shipping Notice (ASN) is an electronic transmission from a vendor to a customer advising them that product they ordered is ready for pick-up.

Monday afternoon and the plant got the parts on Wednesday. The real problem seems to be that some knucklehead saw eight skids of hinges coming from us and since the boxes were the same size and the part numbers looked similar he just clicked the scanner eight times on the same box when in reality he had four boxes of 800s and four boxes of 801s. Right hand hinges, left hand hinges, what's the difference, right? Anyhow, the crisis is over, and everything is under control. I'll let Mack know."

Wonder Woman was out of the room almost before Scott could say, "Thanks, good job!" after her. Dave found himself looking out the door after her. *What was it*, he wondered, *that people say after a superhero leaves the scene of a rescue?* The only phrase he could think of was, "Who was that masked man?" but knew that was the wrong cultural reference.

When he turned around, Scott and Ken were grinning at Dave's reaction to the woman who had just entered the room and left so abruptly. He felt as if they expected him to say something, so he said the first thing that came to his mind. Looking at Ken, then at Scott, all he could get out was "I think I would really like working here!"

Chapter 5

Friends

Monday, May 22, 1989

With ten days between accepting the job offer and her first day at work, Marie busied herself preparing for her big first day. This included piecing together five days of work clothes. She knew her "Mom" clothes would not do for Fairlane's work environment. Her new boss wore a business suit to her three interviews and Kathy Bader, the IT Manager, wore an expensive-looking camel jacket. Marie's two interview suits and three church dresses would have to do until she could invest her first paycheck in more clothes.

She also wondered about working in a company that employed 250 men and only 26 women. Kathy, who would occupy the office next to Marie's, listed the other women during her second interview. In the plant office, Denise Bridges handled production control. Stacey D'Angelo was the administrative assistant for John Anderson and the sales staff. There were five clerical staff in the accounting bullpen and all the rest worked at the Livonia Plant, mostly doing assembly. At the end of her orientation, Scott intended to reassign the payroll clerk and the receptionist to work for Marie and the accounts receivable and payable clerks to the new assistant controller leaving Debbie, Kathy, Marie and the new assistant controller working for him.

Concern about "fitting in" left Marie apprehensive. She recently passed her 42nd birthday. No one else looked much over 30. Some clerks appeared barely out of high school. Would they share interests? Scott explained someone would take her out to lunch every day the first week. Marie would eat with Scott and Kathy on her first day, but what would she do after that?

Marie knew few women as impressive at Kathy Bader. Smart, attractive, fashionable, obviously well educated, confident and not afraid to speak her mind, Marie observed that even during the interview process, Scott listened when Kathy spoke. They acted more like a compatible married couple than co-workers. Perhaps Scott and Kathy's common upper middle-class northern suburbs upbringings gave them a connection.

Like Marie, Debbie grew up in a blue-collar downriver suburb, except without the restraining influences of Marie's Catholic upbringing. Debbie described herself as a party girl, despite three years of marriage. Marie wondered how Debbie would react if she knew Jack remained Marie's first and only lover. She resolved never to let the subject enter the conversation. Debbie did not have Kathy's education, or confidence, but Marie knew she possessed a quick mind.

Much to her relief, Kathy and Debbie went out of their way to make Marie feel at home. Kathy explained, "Most of the guys go out to lunch every day. The trouble is," she said, ticking off the points on her fingers, "most of the time it takes an hour, there aren't many healthy places to eat and the work waits until you get back. Debbie and I normally bring a salad or leftovers and eat in the lunchroom. Everybody eats in shifts because the table only seats six people. If you'd like to join us about twelve-thirty, we'd love to have you eat with us."

Marie found it comforting she would have friends at work.

Chapter 6

Kathy Bader

Monday, June 5, 1989

On the first Monday in June, Dave Johnson parked his car in front of Fairlane Tool for the first time as an employee. While he saw several open parking spaces close to the front door, he figured they must belong to someone specific because no one parked there even though no names appeared on any parking space. He parked opposite the building near the street leaving one empty space between his car and the last one in that row.

Dave's car now had air conditioning and he felt considerably more confident and composed than two weeks earlier. He would have about a thirty-minute drive since he moved from Grand Rapids to live with his girlfriend, Lauren, in Farmington Hills.

As he walked toward the door, he saw a red Mercury Sable pull into the second parking spot right of the front door. "I'm glad I didn't park there," Dave thought. Scott Mackenzie got out of the driver's side and extended his hand.

"Good morning. Welcome aboard."

"Thanks," Dave said. "I parked over there. Is that O.K.?"

"Just about anywhere is fine. We keep the spot to the right of the door for John Anderson, but otherwise it's first come, first served."

Dave thought employees were obviously reserving Scott's spot too. Maybe there were others. He vowed to continue to park where he was until he could observe where everyone regularly parked.

As they walked in the door, Dave noticed that this was the first time he had seen his new boss when his clothing was not at least partially disarrayed.

Scott began to talk in the parking lot as Dave followed, leading him to an empty office in the northwest corner of the accounting area and inviting him to drop off his briefcase. Dave's new office was not large, perhaps ten by fourteen feet. Like most of the building's offices, it had a wooden door with a glass window in the upper half. All the furnishings appeared used, but in good condition, except for the computer monitor and personal computer fresh out of the box.

Scott paused only briefly to unlock his own office door in the accounting area's north side. He gave Dave a new-in-the-box blue and white ceramic Fairlane coffee mug while picking up a faded mug advertising the nearby Village Ford car dealership for himself.

While Scott still wore the blue pinstriped jacket, Dave noted that his boss had unbuttoned his collar and loosened his tie, which was already askew.

Full coffee cups in hand from the break room, they returned to Dave's office to talk about the first day plan. This choice of location struck Dave as unusual since most bosses would choose to put themselves in the "power" seat behind their own desk. Scott seemed perfectly comfortable sitting in one of Dave's visitor chairs.

Scott got right down to business. "It is a long-standing company practice that every new team member participates in a four-week orientation program providing the skills and background to do their job."

During his previous visit, Dave spent time with Ken Carpenter, John Anderson, Scott, Debbie Taylor and then Scott again who made the job offer. He knew his first day would begin by talking with Marie Telehowski, the new human resources manager, and then Kathy Bader, the IT manager, whose schedule did not work out two weeks earlier.

After a few minutes talking over coffee, Scott reviewed the orientation plan and took him to see Marie whose office was near the front door.

Marie, he learned, had been with the company exactly two weeks. Management and hourly non-union employees began their orientation with the human resources manager. New production workers received their orientation from a trainer who worked for the plant manager. In this case, Dave discovered, Marie was still working through her own orientation plan and he was the first person she would orient. Since Marie had never done an orientation before, Scott sat in Marie's office with both of them.

"The ritual," Scott said, "is that we schedule you to meet two to four people a day the first week. Each meeting is supposed to begin by getting to know about the people you will work with. Thus, you'll probably exchange ten-minute versions of your life story. Very often, we will arrange for the person you meet to teach you something such as what their responsibilities are and how you normally interface with their job function. In this case, Marie is going to make sure that you fill out all the required forms, get a copy of the employee manual and tell you about human resources stuff. You get Kathy Bader, the IT manager later, then Marie and Kathy are going to take you to lunch, and you'll spend time with Debbie Taylor, the General Accounting Clerk, and Dean Williams, the Engineering VP after lunch.

"Someone," Scott continued, "will take you to lunch every day this week. On Friday, the three of us will spend the afternoon together since it will be more efficient for me to go over certain things with both of you at the same time. After that, you're on your own for lunch. About a dozen people go out for lunch regularly. I'll give you a list. You would ordinarily be welcome to tag along with any of them. Just stick your head in anybody's door sometime in the morning and ask if they have lunch plans."

Dave liked Marie immediately. Professionally dressed, she was attractive and seemed to have a good sense of humor. Dave was surprised to find she had two teenaged sons and, by the conversation's end, had calculated she must be in her early 40s.

Marie obviously prepared well for the orientation, leading Dave to think Scott coached her on how to conduct these sessions. This might be the test of what she learned. She must have done well because Scott said little during the session and praised the job she did when it was over.

Kathy Bader's office was directly next to Marie's and across from the receptionist desk. Her office was slightly larger than Dave's, but similarly furnished. Dave pulled a black visitor's chair up to her desk. As he sat, he saw a wedding picture sitting on the counter of her modular furniture. Thinking this might be a good way to begin the recommended small talk, he asked about it.

"Did you get married recently?"

She looked around at the picture as anyone does, despite being intimately familiar with the contents of their own office.

"No, actually Mark and I will have our 4th anniversary next month."

"What does he do?"

"He's a real estate agent. He has a marketing degree but found that he could make more money selling real estate than working at an ad agency."

"Did you meet in college?"

"No, I met him at my cousin's wedding. Mark was Scott's college roommate, which is how we all know each other. Three years ago, I was looking for a job at the same time Scott was looking for an IT manager, so here I am."

Like Marie, Kathy was professionally dressed, wearing a tan jacket, white blouse and black slacks. She wore large brown tortoise shell framed glasses, had her brown hair up in the back and held in place with a tooled leather hairpiece through which she pushed a chopstick-like piece of wood. He guessed she was about 30. Dave noted that she wore a small, brass "W" pin on her lapel.

"Did you go to Western?[2]"

"Oh," Kathy said, adjusting its orientation. "No, I went to Michigan."

Getting a good look at her face, Dave had the distinct feeling that he had met her before. Scott had scheduled him to meet her during his last interview, but that meeting hadn't worked out.

"You look familiar to me," he said. "Have we crossed paths someplace before?"

"About two weeks ago. You were with Ken Carpenter in Scott's office. We didn't get introduced, but you were sitting in the chair by the door."

---

[2] Western Michigan University in Kalamazoo.

"Wonder Woman?" Dave almost blurted it out.

"I had my contacts in that day," Kathy added.

"Right, that was probably it." Dave added, still wondering why she seemed to be wearing a costume two weeks ago.

Dave would have liked to find out more about Kathy, but she got down to business quickly. "What software do you know?"

"Lotus, WordStar, Word Perfect and I've had some experience with some general ledger packages," Dave replied.

"Well, that's a good start," she said. We're converting from Pro Write and Framework IV to a Microsoft world, so you'll have to learn to use Excel and Word. I understand they're similar to the packages you already know. I'll get you a password and give you access to all the accounting modules so you can start exploring on your own. We haven't implemented the purchasing and receiving modules yet, because we're still evaluating bar code scanners, but have that scheduled for the end of the year. Your orientation plan should include tutorials in all the accounting software modules. I see you start with Debbie and accounts payable this afternoon. All the software documentation is over there," she said, pointing at two shelves of books.

The lower shelf contained perhaps fifteen to twenty soft cover books with yellow and white covers whose spines bore software module names. On the upper shelf were user manuals for other software. Dave estimated he was looking at five linear feet of computer system documentation.

"It looks like I have a lot to learn," he said.

Chapter 7

Dean Williams

Dave's lunch with Kathy and Marie was fun. Despite his attempt to talk business, by the end of lunch they knew he met Lauren when she posted on the Ball State "ride board," they grew up six blocks apart in Goshen, Indiana, but had never met in high school and where they went on their first date. They knew more about their relationship than he had ever felt comfortable telling anybody in his previous job.

Scott assigned Debbie to teach Dave about the AP software since she had once done the job for 3 years and had a deep understanding of how the accounting modules interacted. On several occasions when she couldn't remember a technical accounting term, she substituted terms from sex or football, causing them both to laugh.

It surprised him that the hour and a half they spent together went so quickly. At first, he thought talking to four people in one day would feel over-scheduled, but he left Debbie's cubicle feeling ready to talk with one more person.

Dave climbed the south stairway to the upper floor central hallway past the offices of John Anderson and the sales staff. Cubicles with CAD[3] workstations lined the engineering bullpen's west wall. Two long conference tables sat between the cubicles and the east windows. Part drawings covered one of them and quality control manager Terry Delaney and two engineers were having a lively discussion about them.

---

[3] Computer-Aided Design

Dean Williams, the company's VP - Engineering, had the corner office in the building's southeast corner, directly above Ken's office, though Dean's office was twice as big. Dean's working desk faced away from the door where he could look out both his office's south and east windows. As Dave knocked on the open door, he could see Dean's profile as he sat at his desk. He judged Dean to be in his mid-40s with dark-framed glasses and dark hair, graying at the temples. He was in the process of copying a number from a Hewlett-Packard engineering calculator. Dean swiveled around on his chair when he heard Dave's knock.

Like Anderson, Dean had a separate round table for meeting with guests and invited Dave to take a seat. Dean wheeled his own high-backed chair over to the small round table.

Dean smiled, "I guess we're supposed to learn a little about each other and then I'm supposed to teach you about hinges. Scott asked me to try to avoid overwhelming you so other people will tell you about our other products later."

Dave saw some family pictures on the wall and asked about the largest one.

"So, you have two children and like to camp?"

Dave quickly learned the picture showed Dean's wife Carol; their daughter, Brenda, who was about to graduate from high school; and their son Kyle, who was just finishing eighth grade. The photo showed a backpacking trip to Isle Royale.

"Where is Isle Royale?" Dave asked.

Dean explained that Isle Royale was a National Park in the west end of Lake Superior, closer to Canada than the United States.

"Then why is it ours?" Dave asked.

"According to one story I heard, at the time the diplomats negotiated the treaty to end the American Revolution, they thought there were two big islands out there. They drew the border between them. By the time the Canadians figured out that only one island existed, the Americans were already mining copper on it."

Dave learned that Dean and Scott were both avid outdoorsmen and their families sometimes spent weekends together and had once gone skiing together at Lake Tahoe. Dean was building a wooden canoe that he hoped to have ready for their annual trip down the Pine River near Cadillac in August.

The conversation was easy and lively and in twenty minutes Dave and Dean learned a lot about each other. It was Dean who changed the subject.

"So, I'm supposed to teach you about hinges. Let's go look at a parts board."

During the interview process, Dave had seen a parts board in the quality control office that displayed an example of every current part. The wall between the sales and engineering departments had a pegboard wall devoted to just hinges. No two hinges looked alike and many were vastly different from any of the others.

Dean began, "Automotive hinges look nothing like the door hinges on your home, which just have a simple pivot point. Sometimes automotive hinges are simple, too. Dean took a simple assembly off the parts board and handed it to Dave. It was two stampings held together with a rivet. Dean said, "We make the stampings, they get plated and then our Livonia plant puts them together with a spin rivet. Have Don show you this process when you go up there.

"On a car, we can't always put the hinges where we want. Thus, the hood may have to lift in both the back and the front to clear the windshield wiper blades. In such situations, we use a 4-bar hinge." Dean took another part off the parts board featuring four stampings riveted into a trapezoidal shape.

Dean showed Dave an obsolete Chrysler hinge with a huge clock spring to provide lift assist. Another huge trunk hinge featured a tube bent into a sickle shape. "Not our design," Dean said. "We call this a luggage crusher because of what it can do to your bags."

"Help me understand," Dave asked, "what gives us a competitive advantage in hinges."

"Great question. I designed some hinges at Ford when John hired me, but I was far from an expert. One of the first things I did was go to a junk yard and ask them to give me a hinge of every recent German and Japanese car they had. It quickly dispelled the myth of German engineering for me. What they were doing was obviously inferior to our state-of-the-art at Ford. I'll show you."

Dean rummaged in a tall cabinet full of parts and pulled out a two-bar hinge whose rivet had been crudely deformed with an "X" shaped tool. Dave instantly understood how opening a hood with this hinge would not have a smooth feel.

Dean continued, "On the other hand, I discovered something very important from the Japanese." He handed Dave another hinge from the file cabinet. "Look at these two tabs."

Two bars of the hinge had tabs that stuck out about a half inch, oriented at ninety degrees from each other and separated by a quarter inch gap. "What are they?" Dave asked.

"Hood catchers," Dean responded.

"Hood catchers?"

"In a car crash, you can't have the hood sheer the hinge pivot point; go through the windshield and decapitate the driver. That would be bad for product liability claims. Some cars have separate hooks that fit into slots under the hood. This subtle little design helps the hood buckle in a front-end collision and is a lot cheaper for the car maker."

Dave was running the numbers through his head. He had never seen a hood catcher but imagined they would cost fifty cents each and another dollar to install. Since you would need two of them per car, Dean was describing a $3 savings per vehicle, far less than the small extra material cost to use a wider piece of metal to add the tabs.

Dean continued, "Today, except for the cheapest cars, gas cylinders provide lift assist for both hoods and trunks. We're trying to integrate the hood catchers and lift assist all in the hinge assembly. Since nobody else is doing that today, we've got a big opportunity in this market."

Returning to his own office at 4:30 pm, Dave's head was beginning to feel a little numb from all the information thrown at him. As he sat at his desk filling out the forms Marie gave him, Scott walked in and sat down in one of his visitor's chairs.

"So, how did the first day go?"

"It was a lot to absorb all at once," Dave replied.

"Tomorrow won't be quite so hectic," Scott said. "You get most of the afternoon to familiarize yourself with the computer system."

Dave said, "I see I have Jimmy Mack Jones at 8:30."

"He's the plant manager. I think I introduced you briefly during your first interview. You probably remember him, the large black man that's roughly the size of a grizzly bear."

Dave couldn't help but remember him.

Scott continued, "Mack's in charge of operations. That means manufacturing, shipping, material handling and purchasing. For example, Ken Carpenter works for Mack. He played tackle at Eastern, so John met him through his football connections. Great guy, you'll want to have him walk you through the reports he uses to manage the plant."

"Is his office up above quality control?" Dave asked.

"Yes, he's out on the floor a lot but is usually easy to find." Dave made a note about where to find Mack on his orientation plan.

"Tomorrow you're having lunch with our three sales reps, Bud Pierce, Ray Peltier and Michael Anderson. Bud and Ray are the two guys upstairs with gray hair, so you can't miss them. Bud is the thinner contemplative one and Ray is the outgoing joker with the beer belly. Michael is the tall, blond guy who looks like the fashion model."

Dave was sure that all three had come by to introduce themselves. He had met so many people in such a short period that he struggled to remember all the names. Already he felt like a member of the team. He found it hard to believe he had learned so much about the business in just one day.

Chapter 8

Tool and Die

June 6, 1989

As Dave walked toward his office on his second morning, Kathy came through the door that separated the break room from Accounting wearing a white sailor suit including bell-bottom trousers with two rows of buttons and a pullover U.S. Navy jersey with insignia bearing a red cross and three chevrons on the sleeve.

"Good morning, sailor," was all Dave could manage to say.

Kathy stopped. "Thank you. The pants are new, but the shirt was my father's. I'm wearing it today in his honor."

"Where did he serve?" Dave asked.

"Europe. He was a Navy corpsman on an LST evacuating the wounded during the Normandy invasion. Today is the 45th anniversary." Kathy continued down the hall but stopped, turned and laughed. "He was wearing this shirt in Baltimore on VJ Day. He says he'd never kissed so many girls in his life."

Dave arrived in the manufacturing offices at 8:28 a.m. to learn that Jimmy Mack Jones was out in the plant. Manufacturing management occupied a two-story modular structure sitting almost directly in the middle of the factory with large windows giving a 360-degree view of operations. Production Control and supervisory personnel occupied the second floor with Quality Control below.

"You must be Dave Johnson." A large black woman with a friendly smile rose from her desk and extended her hand as he entered the room. "I'm Denise Bridges. Jimmy said he'd be back in a couple of minutes. You can go in his office and sit down if you want. Or, I can offer you a cup of coffee."

"Coffee sounds good."

Denise nodded toward the back wall where a white coffeemaker and a sleeve of Styrofoam cups sat on a black metallic bookcase. Dave poured coffee into a cup, but upon finding only a single creamer-encrusted communal spoon, he decided to drink his coffee black.

Turning back toward Denise he asked, "So what do you do here?"

Denise faced away from him, looking at the numbers on her computer screen. She removed her glasses, allowing them to hang from a pair of pink peeper-keepers and swiveled her chair to face him directly. "Production control; I handle scheduling, production data recording and inventory."

"How long have you been with Fairlane?"

"Six years in September."

Before Dave could learn any more about Denise, they heard Mack climbing the metal staircase leading to the production office. The thump of the stamping presses grew appreciably as he opened the door. During Dave's first interview, Scott introduced him. Though Mack had done little more than shaken Dave's hand, meeting him had been memorable. Standing at nearly 6'5", he was an imposing figure. With broad shoulders and huge meaty hands, Dave estimated this man was somewhere north of 280 pounds. His huge brown nose was abnormally flat, and his big smile gave the impression he was an immensely likable character.

Mack poured a coffee for himself and they chatted in his office. Dave learned that he grew up in Detroit, played defensive tackle at Eastern Michigan University, had a short career with the Ottawa Rough Riders and Mack wasn't really his middle name. The song "Jimmy Mack" had been popular when he was in high school. He had five children and lived in Southfield.

"Scott wants you to teach me about workflow today," Dave said.

"Got some ear plugs?" Mack responded. Dave produced a still clean pair from his pocket. Mack nodded his head. "Good," he said and then set down his empty coffee cup. Dave followed the big man down the stairs into the factory. "We'll start at the beginning," Mack said, pointing to the open doors in the building's northeast corner.

Eight 30 x 48 inch dry-erase boards occupied the upper north wall showing descriptions and machine numbers of Fairlane's eight primary stamping presses written in red. Lists of parts each machine ran were on each board written in smaller black letters. In front of each board were columns of steel coils, laid flat on wooden pallets. Some coils were only an inch and a half wide. Others might be 30 inches wide. The thinner coils were sometimes stacked as many as eight per pallet. A wide coil might occupy a pallet alone. Stacked pallets might reach eight or more feet in the air.

"What does this mean?" Dave asked, pointing to codes hand-written on each coil with durable yellow letters.

"The first line is the part number. This is a Ford part. We make hood hinges that Ford calls E9TB-16800 and 801-AA. E is the decade, 9 is the year, T means an F-Series pick-up truck, B means Body Engineering, the Ford office responsible for the specification, 16800 means a right-handed hood hinge and 16801 is a left-handed hood hinge. AA is the engineering change level. We use a variation of that number. We get rid of the E and B and reverse the order of the T and the 9. Thus, this number, T9-16880-AA is a component of those Ford hinges."

Dave took notes as Mack continued the explanation.

"This is the coil weight in pounds pointing at #5,885 and 9156A means the first lot of this material on the 156th day of 1989, which would be yesterday," pointing at the various components of the lot number.

Dave looked at another pallet of steel and saw a slash and another number following the coil weight. He asked, "Does this mean the weight is for five coils?"

"Yes, it wouldn't be practical for us to weigh each coil on the skid individually, and we don't need that information. Besides, they would have slit all five coils from the same master coil and thus they would weigh about the same. If we only used four coils, we wouldn't even need to reweigh the one that remained. We could just divide by five."

As the morning break ended, Mack was describing the operation of a secondary stamping press when its operator, a thin black man with some gray around his temples, returned to his workstation. "Let me introduce you. Dave Johnson, this is Leroy Johnson. Leroy is one of the few people still here from Silent Tool."

Leroy said, "It's good to meet you, Mr. Johnson."

Leroy removed one work glove as Dave reached out to shake his hand. "Just call me Dave please."

"All right Mr. Dave."

Mack noted, "With the same last name, perhaps you're somehow related."

It didn't seem likely, as Dave Johnson was as pale as Leroy Johnson was dark, but they both laughed at the thought.

"OK then, you can call me Cousin Leroy."

Mack explained that Leroy had six children, four of whom were in college and two others who were high school honor students at Cass Tech as the press operator beamed with pride.

After they left the man, Dave asked, "Leroy is much older than any of the other secondary press operators. Is there a story there?"

Mack explained that Leroy had a learning disability. He couldn't read very well and was probably dyslexic. "We've tried to teach him how to do other jobs, but each time it hasn't gone well. He's good at this job, is satisfied with it, and so this is what he does." Three hours and nine pages of notes later, Dave felt he had received a helpful manufacturing education. Sometimes questions from production operators or quality control personnel interrupted the lesson plan. However, Mack invited Dave to listen to every conversation and tried to make it a learning experience. Equally valuable, Dave thought, was that he had made a friend whom he could call on any time he had questions about production.

Bud Pierce was the only person in the Sales Department when Dave arrived at ten minutes of noon.

"Hi, Dave! Ray and Mike visited customers this morning, but they'll meet us at the restaurant. Let's go."

Bud led Dave through Accounting and out the front door. Since Bud wore a suit jacket, Dave grabbed his as they passed his office. Dave got into Bud's company car, an almost new silver Mercury Sable.

"So, what has Scott told you about the Sales Department?" Bud asked

"Not much," Dave replied.

"Well, then I guess I can start at the beginning. John handled sales himself when he bought out Silent Tool in 1974. He hired Ray in 1980 to handle Chrysler and I joined the company in '82 to help with Ford. His brother Mike has been here since he graduated from State. Mike worked for Dean Williams as an engineering assistant and with me on Ford sales for about three. I know you've met Ray. Have you met Mike?"

"Yes, briefly," Dave replied. "He's the tall blond guy, right?"

"Yes."

At the restaurant, they found Ray reading the **Detroit Free Press** at a table facing the door. "What's going on in the world?" Bud asked.

"I was reading this article about a double homicide in Detroit. According to the story, this woman, Twila, had a live-in boyfriend, Lamont, who may have been a small-time drug dealer. It seems she suspected Lamont of fooling around and warned him about what she'd do if she ever caught him. So, she arrives home early to find him with a woman who may have been one of his customers trading drugs for sex. His gun was on the dresser, so she shot them both. It seems the prosecutor is sympathetic to her circumstances, particularly in view of Lamont's profession and may let Twila plea bargain to manslaughter."

As Ray told the story, Michael Anderson walked in the door.

"Hi guys. Dave, good to see you again."

Ray continued, "So the moral of the story should interest all of you, particularly Mike."

"The moral of the story?" Bud asked.

"What story?" Mike asked.

"A woman shot her cheating boyfriend in Detroit," Ray explained.

"Oh yeah, I read the same story this morning," Mike confirmed.

"OK," Bud said. "Now that we're all on the same page, what's the moral of the story?"

"Tool & Die."

"Tool and Die?" Dave asked.

"Yeah, like my wife tells me, 'keep your tool in your pants, or you're gonna die.' That's good advice for you, young man," Ray said, looking at Michael.

"Fortunately, I've never had a woman that pissed off at me," Michael said, obviously uncomfortable with the discussion's direction. Bud quickly changed the subject and Dave found the rest of lunch considerably more jovial.

An hour later, the four men walked across the restaurant parking lot to the three cars they came in. As Dave fastened his seat belt, he probed Bud about the lunch conversation's early uncomfortableness.

"Tool and die. I think that point went right by me."

Bud reflected about how to explain the exchange to Dave, holding up his right index finger to indicate he was forming his words.

"As you can tell, Michael is tall and very good looking. Women sometimes throw themselves at him. Usually, he handles it very well. However, sometimes he doesn't. Ray isn't always tactful. Mike is divorced right now. Somebody will probably tell you the story sometime, but I wouldn't feel comfortable being that person."

Chapter 9

Friday Afternoon

June 9, 1989

"I could think of worse places to spend a Friday afternoon," Scott said, as he, Dave and Marie settled into seats at a glass-topped table near the Fairlane Club's outdoor pool. Less than two miles from Ford World Headquarters, and next to Fairlane Mall, the club featured athletic facilities, meeting rooms, banquet facilities, and two restaurants. The Andersons, Scott and a few key managers had memberships they used almost exclusively for business. Since none of them lived near Dearborn, no one in the company regularly used the athletic facilities.

Scott rarely ate in the Club's formal dining room preferring the sports bar, which offered poolside seating from Memorial Day to Labor Day.

Scott left his jacket and tie in the car, expressing his relief to remove the tie and Dave followed his boss's lead.

Marie did not remove her suit jacket as they left the car, but did so when she saw they were sitting poolside. Dave found himself looking at Marie's chest as she took off her jacket, noting that she was wearing a white lace bra under her blouse. He turned his eyes toward Scott to avoid the possibility she might notice him gazing at her chest. More than once during his first week on the job, Dave had found himself looking at her chest. He thought it seemed wrong to notice the figure of a woman who was his senior by seventeen years. After all, he thought, *she's only five years younger than my mother!* As Dave averted his eyes, he noticed Scott looking at her, too, and Scott smiled as he turned toward Dave, leading Dave to wonder if they had been doing the same thing.

Marie alone chose to sit outside the umbrella's shadow, arching her back to the sky to expose her face to the June sun's glory. This time Dave was positive Scott was looking at her chest and the two men exchanged knowing looks. As a brunette, Marie could get away with sitting in the sun, while redheaded Scott never tanned and Dave still had a distinctive accountant's winter pallor.

As Scott instructed, Dave and Marie each brought a pen and paper to take notes.

Dave looked around the pool. The people did not exactly look like the poolside scenery of a James Bond movie. In one corner sat an obviously pregnant woman dangling her feet in the water while her toddler played on the shallow end steps. Another woman in a turquoise one-piece bathing suit supervised two children who were perhaps 6 and 8. When a white-haired man joined them, Dave concluded these were their grandchildren.

A waiter in black slacks, vest and a white shirt took their drink order and left menus. Following his boss's lead, Dave ordered a Stroh's beer while Marie ordered white wine. Ignoring the menu, Scott began with a story:

"Dan Thompson, my predecessor at Fairlane, was a hard partying blue-collar type who often rode his motorcycle to work. Not a typical accountant! All the clerks loved him. The first time I went to lunch with Jack Porter, who was, and still is, our bank loan officer, we ate in the main dining room upstairs. I'll take you there some time when the weather isn't so nice. It has a formal, stuffy atmosphere, but the food and service are excellent. As we walked out of the dining room, Jack thanked me for lunch and remarked it wasn't the kind of place Dan usually took him. I asked where they went and he told me those places had entertainment. In fact, later I met the bank branch manager who told me about going out to lunch with Dan and running into one of Dan's former wives, he had four, who was one of the entertainers...."

At that point, the waiter came with their drinks. Dave wasn't sure there was more to the story, but since Scott suggested they look at the menu, he decided not to ask. Scott quickly looked at his menu and set it aside. Dave figured he should follow suit and made a quick decision. Marie chose more deliberately, and Scott sipped his beer patiently while waiting for her full attention.

"Before I start talking about the scheduled agenda items, there are a few things you both should know about me." Marie immediately noticed that Scott talked in a more open, tentative tone than before.

"I've been doing this job for six years. I think I understand the accounting, finance and information systems issues pretty well, but I also know that I'm learning new things all the time. One thing I'm just really beginning to learn is the people part of the job. Some people issues I just can't see, and when I do see them, I don't know how to handle them. Thus, if either of you see something that you don't think I'm reacting to appropriately please, come into my office, close the door and explain what you see, because the biggest favor you can do for me is to tell me when I'm wrong."

As Scott talked, Dave listened, alternating between looking at Scott and looking contemplatively at his own hands. Dave responded, "We didn't get into accounting because we were good with people. I struggle with the same issues." He looked at Scott and they both looked at Marie.

She took a sip of her wine, then said, "I guess I'm the opposite. Sometimes I focus too much on how people feel. My challenge will be that most of what I know about Human Resources so far is from a book."

Scott said, "We'll be fine as a team if we support each other. Well, at least part of a team. Kathy and the rest of our three departments are important resources, too."

Scott explained they were going to spend the entire Friday afternoon away from the office, trying to get Dave and Marie more deeply immersed in the company's plans.

"The name of the game right now is scalability. We have enough new work in the pipeline that, barring some major, unforeseen event, will take us to $70 million within two years. We have 32 parts in the new Ford Escort, 26 parts on the upcoming Econoline van, parts on the new Lincoln Mark VIII, the Mercury Villager and a couple of other vehicles. We just completed a major update in our computer software, but keeping together an infrastructure capable of supporting that kind of growth is going to be a challenge."

The waiter reappeared and took orders before Scott continued.

"We just bought a series of videotape training material for machine operators. Marie, a big part of your job will be working with Jimmy and Brian, our manufacturing trainer, to make sure we can bring new production workers up to speed efficiently but without taking any shortcuts that would jeopardize quality or safety.

"Dave, I have to get myself out of day-to-day Accounting Department operations. Your key responsibilities initially are cost accounting and the financial systems at the Livonia plant, but as soon as you feel you're ready to take on more, there's a lot more for you to do.

"John and I believe in a relatively flat organizational structure. Marie, did you bring that updated organizational chart?" he asked.

"Yes, I have three copies," she said, pulling them from a manila folder under her pad of paper, giving one each to Dave and Scott.

Scott continued, "You'll notice that John has eight direct reports: Mack, Dean, me, the three sales reps, Stacy, and Don Kelley, the plant manager in Livonia who isn't shown. There are a couple of reasons for a flat organizational structure. First, it reduces the amount of bureaucracy and second it is almost impossible to micromanage if you have more than seven people working for you.

"Technically, all eight people in administration, including the five clerks, report to me. However, that can't last much longer if we grow. After her orientation period is up, Marie will give the payroll clerk and receptionist most of their direction. Dave, you will do the same for our accounts payable and accounts receivable clerks and the office manager in Livonia. There, of course, the direct reporting relationship is with Don Kelley; but effectively we're providing the overall direction as to what goes on in accounting up there.

"Everybody in administration is accustomed to being coached, rather than supervised, so you might as well get used to it from the start."

Back at Fairlane Tool, Jimmy looked over the two 4' x 8' white boards containing the day's press schedule. The lack of red entries meant that no one would work on Saturday, a fact everyone knew by Wednesday morning. On Monday, the plant would shift to its usual 6:30 a.m. to 3 p.m. summer schedule. In a few hours, he would be in his Southfield backyard, grilling steaks with a cold blue and gold can of Stroh's in his hand.

In the office, Debbie was helping the accounts payable clerk who had fallen behind the weekly accounting department schedule due to the Memorial Day holiday. She set a stack of payment documentation on top of the four-drawer lateral file cabinet. Filing was the perfect task for the last few hours on a Friday.

Down the hall, Kathy Bader sipped the last iced tea from the jug she brought on Monday. After work, she would don a Detroit Tigers jersey and see the game with her husband Mark, Scott and Mary Mackenzie.

John Anderson returned late from lunch at his mother's home in Dearborn. He checked his few messages and seeing there was nothing that could not wait until Monday, called his wife, Barbara, and left early for the weekend. Anderson loved a day when everything ran smoothly.

Lauren gave Dave a long deep kiss as he walked into their apartment. Despite having the same address for more than a week, Dave had not seen Lauren since Monday morning as she had been out-of-town working on a school district audit in mid-Michigan. She had beaten him home by six minutes and was still wearing a beige skirt and white blouse from her day at the client. She led him into the bedroom to change. They carefully hung up their suits before meeting between their bi-fold door closets for another long kiss. Pausing for a moment, she unhooked her front-hook bra and flung it to the chair in the corner. "It feels great to get that off!" Soon, the neatly made bed was in shambles and she lay naked on top of him underneath only a sheet.

When Dave awoke, it was almost 7 p.m. and Lauren was no longer beside him in bed. Putting on some clothes, he found her in the kitchen wearing gym shorts and a t-shirt cutting chicken and vegetables to make stir-fry. "I'm glad you're up, I'm starved," she said as she popped a piece of bell pepper in her mouth and washed it down with a gulp of white wine.

"I'm not surprised you have an appetite." Neither of them was quite comfortable talking about sex yet, but they had both stopped blushing when the conversation alluded to the topic. Another wine glass sat next to the bottle of slightly fizzy Italian wine and Dave poured himself half a glass. He hadn't really acquired a taste for wine, yet, but since Lauren did not drink beer, he drank wine when she did.

Lauren had set places for dinner on the black metal café table on their tiny 2nd floor balcony. Their view faced east overlooking the common area adjoining six of the twelve buildings in their apartment complex. A few bites into the meal, Lauren asked Dave to tell her about his new job.

"So far, it's been a great place to work! The people are really nice, and I've learned an unbelievable amount in just a week. At the end of each day, I feel almost overwhelmed with the amount of new things they have thrown at me. I know this can't last forever, but for right now, it is one heck of a ride and I feel lucky to be on board."

Chapter 10

September Song

Michael Anderson had no idea why the name on the back of his 45-foot Stevens sailboat read **September Song**. He bought the boat from an insurance company after lightning hit it docked in Chicago. The lightning strike fried most of the electrical systems and caused several curious deformities in the lead keel and fiberglass hull. The previous owner took his insurance proceeds and bought a new boat. Michael was glad to be able to purchase the eight-year old boat for a small fraction of its original price.

The trip to sail **September Song** back to Detroit with three of Michael's sailing buddies stood as a landmark in Michael and Laurie Anderson's two-year old marriage. Laurie's previous sailing experience consisted of short sails on relatively calm Lake St. Clair. Two hours out of Chicago she began vomiting uncontrollably on Lake Michigan's rough waters, spending most of the next 24 hours in her bunk. When not below deck, she occupied herself by criticizing Michael for the boat purchase. Before they reached the trip's halfway point, **September Song** made an unscheduled stop at a Traverse City marina. Laurie took a cab to a local hotel and caught a plane back to Detroit the next morning.

From that day forward, Laurie rarely came onboard when **September Song** left the dock. Sometimes she met Michael for drinks and dinner at the club after a race on Lake St. Clair, but she only went out on the water in very calm weather or when the social occasion demanded it.

In the summer, Michael often went to the boat after lunch on Friday afternoon. He might share a beer with other boat owners, do routine maintenance, or sometimes just enjoy a peaceful afternoon nap.

One such Friday afternoon precipitated the Anderson's divorce. Laurie reconnected with two of her sorority sisters at a wedding and arranged to meet them for lunch at the club a few weeks later, neglecting to tell Michael. She reserved a window table overlooking the water. Laurie was showing off. She didn't have to actually brag outright. The club, the expensive new white dress, the matching white hat and the subtle mention of their boat at the end of the dock said it all for her.

After insisting lunch was her treat, Laurie suggested she show her friends the boat. Walking down the dock, the three pretty, young women in sundresses stood out among the casually attired middle-aged and older boaters. The sight of a woman's beach tote on **September Song's** deck and the sound of giggling from down below told Laurie and her friends more than they wanted to know. Her new white hat blowing off into the dirty water completed her humiliation as she confronted her cheating husband.

Laurie Anderson filed for divorce within the week and their young marriage officially ended a few weeks into 1989.

Chapter 11

Running the Numbers

Wednesday, June 21, 1989

"Good Morning!" Dave stood at Scott's office door with a cup of coffee. "My 30 Day Plan says that you're going to teach me about budgeting this morning."

"Yes," Scott said. "Follow me to the break room so we can talk while I get coffee, too." In the break room, Ray and Michael were just draining the Bunn coffee maker's right-hand pot. The other pot, which Dave had started only a minute before, was actively filling. "I'll take care of it," Scott said to the sales guys. "We're going to have to wait a couple of minutes for the other pot anyhow."

Scott talked as he rinsed out the pot, filled it and poured it into the back of the coffee maker. "I'm guessing you didn't have much exposure to budgets during your two years in public accounting."

"Absolutely none at all."

"I'm sure you'll catch on quickly."

"One thing I wondered," Dave asked, "was how did we end up with a July 31st fiscal year end? It seems unusual. Most companies who aren't on calendar years would end their fiscal years on an even quarter."

"I don't know, other than 7/31 corresponds pretty well to the auto industry model change-over. They could have made the year end June 30th, but that would have conflicted with when most people in this town want to go on vacation."

Scott filled his cup and they went back into his office, pulling his guest chair around his desk so they both could look at his computer screen.

"We project three years because we work with a three year product launch schedule. We revise roughly quarterly, depending on how much we think things have changed from last time. We don't always revise all three years of projections, but this time we will because we need to add another 12 months. The sales projections come first, but they aren't that hard because we have dependent demand."

"Dependent demand?" Dave asked.

"Yeah, our sales depend on how many vehicles our customers sell."

Scott explained how their Sales Projection model calculated revenue and direct cost using:

- Estimated annual sales for each customer vehicle
- A list of Fairlane parts on each vehicle
- The price of each part
- Each part's materials, labor, purchased part and outside processing cost.

"Our model also apportions sales and costs by month using the expected number of customer assembly plant working days each year. Each customer plant shuts for two weeks in the summer and again for about ten days at Christmas. July and December are always much lower sales than the rest of the year."

Dave could see that this method would generate extremely accurate sales projections as long as the estimates of customer vehicle sales were accurate. Scott showed him a comparison of budget to actual revenue projections for the last six years. The company's sales projections had never been off by more than 2%. "That doesn't mean they can't be off by more," Scott said. "The country could have an economic crisis, a customer might postpone a product launch or the market could just reject a new vehicle. I haven't seen that in six years here, but it could always happen."

The budget model lesson lasted almost three hours. While Dave had never seen a budget model before, he couldn't imagine that models would get much more sophisticated. Even a small volume change to one product would send other changes cascading through direct materials, direct labor, outside processing costs and a long list of payroll related benefits as well as accounts receivable, inventory levels and bank borrowing requirements.

It had never occurred to Dave that anyone would integrate balance sheet and cash flow projections with an income statement budget. No one ever discussed this in business school. It made perfect sense. Scott's big worry for the next few years was getting the money to finance growth and the projections showed the problem vividly. To have enough money, they would have to maintain profitability, productivity and reduce inventory turns. Even then, this kind of growth was likely to make the bank more than a little nervous.

Chapter 12

The Canoe Trip

Saturday August 19, 1989

In his dream, Dave Johnson wandered from classroom to classroom at Ball State trying to find his final exam room. His search grew increasingly urgent because the exam was already underway and he could name neither the subject nor professor he sought. Finally, as students poured into the corridor from every final exam, he rolled over. This simple movement immediately refocused his brain on his current reality. He realized that he was not in his bed and college was more than three years behind him. He and Lauren were in borrowed double sleeping bags and a borrowed tent in a state park campground.

Dave remembered why he was on this trip. Passing through engineering one day, he asked Dean about his canoe-building project. That led to hearing about an upcoming trip Dean planned. Dave said politely, "That sounds like fun," and now he and Lauren lay in a tent along the Pine River, west of Cadillac. He could hear the sound of the moving water only a few yards away.

Four years in Girl Scouts taught Lauren how to put up the tent. An avid outdoorsman, Dean lent them most of the equipment they needed. The tent protected them from the morning dew and two mattress pads cushioned their bodies from the hard ground. Dean's wife, Carol, explained to him how to zip the matching sleeping bags together "for added warmth." *Good advice*, he thought as he turned toward Lauren and felt her body through her flannel pajamas. The nighttime temperature seemed cold for the third weekend in

August. He pulled the sleeping bag over the top of his head to ward off the early morning chill.

It was the tenth year Dean organized the trip. This year included Dean and Carol Williams, their children Brenda, 17, and Kyle, 14, Scott and Mary Mackenzie, Kathy and Mark Bader, and two other couples who were Dean's longtime friends. Lauren had canoed a few times on a lake at Girl Scout camp, but never on a river. That experience beat Dave's since he had hardly ever set foot in any small boat, much less a canoe. In the break room a few days before the trip, he asked Kathy what to expect. She told him she and Mark tipped twice the first time they joined the trip two years earlier. She advised him to prepare for tipping by bringing extra clothes in a dry bag. "If you know you're going to go in and prepare for it, you'll have a good time."

As Dave emerged from the tent, Kathy passed by with a washcloth, towel and a toiletries bag returning from the restrooms. By now, Dave was accustomed to seeing Kathy in costume. Over a gray, long-sleeved T-shirt, she wore green zip-off cargo pants and a short-sleeved, V-necked shirt covered with patches.

"Nice shirt," he said. "Where did you pick that up?"

"The Goodwill, in Livonia," she said. "I think I'm supposed to be a Love Scout," pointing at the heart-shaped badge on her left breast pocket.

"Life Scout," Scott said as he emerged from his tent. "Life is the second highest rank in Scouting." Scott studied the badges on her uniform. "These two are real collector's items," he said, pointing at the patches on her shirt. "Here is the '64 National Jamboree at Valley Forge and this one commemorates Scouting's 50th anniversary."

Dave couldn't believe all three of them were giving Kathy's chest such close inspection.

"Farmington Hills, Troop 179," Scott noted, looking at one of Kathy's shoulders, and "Beaver Patrol," looking at the other. "It's perfect attire for the river."

Scott wore an old gray sweatshirt with the words Youghiogheny River on the front and a river map on the back. The two men walked to the restroom exchanging small talk about the cool morning. When they returned, Scott extracted a long blue and yellow paddle from the back of Mary's Taurus station wagon. As he leaned it against a tree, Dave estimated the paddle was six feet long. "Maize and Blue," Dave commented, recognizing Scott's school colors. Scott extracted a second, much shorter green and white paddle. "Mixed marriage," Scott said, holding Mary's paddle bearing the Michigan State Spartan colors.

When Dave remarked at the foot and a half difference in the paddle length, Scott explained he brought his own six-foot "guide paddle" because most rental paddles were only 4'6" or 5'0" and he had better control with the longer length. Dean joined the conversation explaining that the longer length required greater upper body strength. Williams had once used such a paddle, but went shorter after reaching age 40.

"These guys know what they're doing," Dave thought. "I'm glad somebody does."

Dean posted job assignments. The men would do all the cooking and dishes for the weekend with Scott and Mark Bader making breakfast. While they waited to eat, Dean gave Dave and Lauren a canoeing lesson.

Dean explained that the canoe livery would take them upriver to their put-in point. "We canoe back down here to

Peterson's Bridge. There will be two small bridges before you get to here. The take-out is well marked so you shouldn't miss it. Others from our crew will probably be waiting for you on the shore. But if you get to that concrete bridge over there, you've gone too far."

Dave could see the 325-foot-long bridge well above the trees a few hundred yards to the west. It would be hard to miss.

Since they didn't have their canoe yet, Dean sat Dan and Lauren on either end of the log railing that marked parking spaces. "You should paddle on one side and she should paddle on the other," he explained. "If one of you gets tired, you should both switch sides at the same time. The person in the back steers. If you are in the front," he said, looking at Lauren, "you only need one stroke." He demonstrated a straight stroke with one hand on top of the paddle and the other near the blade. "You'll last longer if you let your torso do the work, instead of your arms." Turning to Dave, he said, "You need three strokes: the same straight stroke, a sweep and a J-stroke."

Dave practiced the straight stroke in the air a few times, and then the sweep. The "J-stroke" seemed a lot more complicated. He understood the stroke was supposed to form the letter "J", but he never quite understood how it turned the boat. It clicked when Dean showed him that the end of the stroke was supposed to push water away from the boat instead of toward the surface of the water. "Just in case," Dean added, "you can always use your paddle like a rudder. Experienced paddlers don't use a rudder, because it slows you down, but if you need it, using a rudder will turn you quickly. The rudder only works if you are moving faster than the river. In canoeing speed means maneuverability. If you are just drifting along, the rudder won't do anything. Thus, if you need to rest, do it on a straight-away, but never do it on a curve or in rapids." The word "rapids" made Dave more than a little nervous.

Dean went over other safety issues and made sure they had a tough, watertight bag for extra clothes "Just in case." Dean added, "Scott and I are always in the last two canoes if anyone needs help." The whole process looked easy to Dave and he looked forward to adding a new skill.

As the lesson completed, Brenda Williams, Dean's daughter emerged from her tent. Dave had seen her recent high school picture on Dean's desk. While her picture made her look very pretty, she was even more attractive in person. Slim and about 5'6", her pale blue eyes were striking in combination with her black hair. Dressed in a red L.L. Bean pullover fleece jacket, she looked very comfortable in the outdoors.

The first few trips had been a "couples" weekend. However, Dean began bringing his children five years before when his then 9-year-old son, Kyle, pleaded to come. The Mackenzie's one and four-year-old daughters were with Mary's mother for the weekend. Dean would paddle with Kyle and his wife Carol with Brenda. Everyone else would canoe as couples.

The van driver, a wiry gray-haired man, drove them to the put-in point at Elm Flats, in a van pulling a canoe trailer. Carol's minivan transported the remainder of the contingent and Dean's wooden canoe. Dave looked out the van window and studied the straight rows of pine trees beside the dirt road, evidence of reforestation decades before. Occasionally, a driveway would leave the main road accompanied by a sign for a "camp." Some camps featured expensive-looking log houses. Others consisted of decrepit old singlewide mobile homes. Often Dave could see nothing more than a pine-needle-covered two-track meandering into the forest with no dwelling visible from the road.

Scott helped the driver with the first canoe, after which Mark and Dave pitched in; quickly setting the boats they needed at the river's edge. Dean and Brenda removed the wood canoe from the top of the minivan. Obviously, she knew what she was doing, cheerfully distributing her family's equipment between two boats without waiting for her father's instructions.

Dave surveyed the river, watching a dry leaf move steadily downstream. The lack of white water relieved him. Still, the water was moving at a strong, steady pace. Scott came up beside him and pointed out some river features. "Stay to the deepest part of the river," he advised. "The inside bank of a curve will be shallower than the outside bank. Sometimes the inside curve will be deep enough to travel, but often it won't. Be careful of any place the water looks rough. It usually means there is an obstacle underneath it. You'll learn how to read the river soon enough. We have a fun stretch of whitewater the last half hour of the trip."

One of Dean's neighbors would take the lead canoe, planning to stop for lunch in about two hours. Scott would bring up the rear. He explained this was a common safety precaution in river canoeing and suggested Dave and Lauren shove off immediately after the neighbor since they were likely to be the slowest boat.

Scott held the middle of Dave's boat steady as Lauren got in. Dave stepped in next. He didn't know what happened, but suddenly he found himself losing his balance and falling over. The weight of his body hitting the gunwale made the whole canoe lurch toward the river's center. Before he knew it, he was sitting on the bottom of a half-foot of cold, moving water. The lower half of his body was wet as well as one arm.

Fortunately, Scott's hold on the canoe was enough to prevent Dave's fall from pitching Lauren into the river, too. His fall alarmed her, but fear turned to sympathy when she found he wasn't hurt. Since he wore a bathing suit for shorts, he decided not to change into his dry clothes right away. Still, he was uncomfortable in the wet bathing suit and the cold air and was glad his sweatshirt was mostly dry.

Dave sat down on a grassy spot and dumped the water out of his soggy old tennis shoes. Lauren provided sympathy while Scott continued to hold the boat in place. Carol Williams rummaged through her dry bag and found a small, well-worn hand towel. Dave used it to dry off his shorts and legs as best he could.

"The Pine has baptized you," Dean observed.

"Gee, that was embarrassing," Dave said.

Dean responded, "Thousands of other people have had unplanned baptisms in the Pine. I tipped the first time and I'm guessing the river has dunked Scott before.

"On a 1969 Boy Scout trip," his boss confirmed, "the only thing to do now is get back in the saddle."

Scott held the boat again and this time gave Dave specific instructions about where to step and how to hold on the gunwales as he entered the canoe. When they were settled, Scott eased the canoe's bow into the current and pushed them off gently.

Dave did not know how fast they moved. He thought they traveled faster than a normal walking pace, but much slower than an all-out run. The first turn would require a sweep stroke. Their canoe began to round the corner on the far side of the curve. The stroke wasn't enough and their canoe crashed into the low-hanging brush hanging out into the water. Lauren ducked, but the branches caught in her long blonde hair and she cried out in pain when a few strands caught in the tree. The canoe hit an outstretched log hard, making a loud metal sound like a baseball bat hitting a 55-gallon metal drum. With the front end stopped by the log, the current grabbed the back end and spun them around. Their canoe was now traveling down the river backwards and Dave had no idea what to do.

Trying to remember what Dean had taught him, Dave held his paddle up against the side of the boat like a rudder, but nothing happened. "Right," he thought. "The boat has to be moving forward for this to work." Instinctively, he pushed his paddle backward against the river and the canoe faced forward. The result was to propel Lauren into overhanging branches along the shore. Catching a tree along the shore, the river turned them backwards a second time.

In the meantime upriver, Brenda and Carol, Kathy and Mark, and Dean's other neighbors launched their boats. Dean and Scott had the only canoes that weren't launched. As they stood on shore, they heard Dave and Lauren's canoe bang against the log. Scott looked down the river in the noise's direction.

"Maybe it wasn't such a good idea for us to let those two paddle together."

"I was just thinking the same thing," Dean responded. "Let's catch up with them and evaluate the situation."

The two canoes paddled side by side, Scott and Mary on the left, Dean and Kyle on the right. Scott turned to Dean to engage him in problem solving. "If we had to put one of our bow people in the stern, who would it be?"

Dean pondered the question.

Mary chimed in "I've been in the stern on a lake."

Dean added, "Brenda has too".

"Then why don't Brenda and I go together?" Mary volunteered.

Scott filled in the rest of the plan. "Then Dave goes with Dean, Lauren goes with me and Kyle goes with Carol.

"That works," Dean said.

As the two back canoes worked out the contingency plan, Carol and Brenda Williams tried to talk Dave and Lauren through the process of getting their canoe facing forward and going down the middle of the river.

"Lauren, stop paddling for a minute," Carol instructed. "Dave, sweep backward on the left hand side of your boat. Okay, Lauren, now paddle on the right."

Carol's instructions saved Dave and Lauren from bouncing off the other shore. Still, they were not out of danger. Blocking the river's left side was a large brush pile and Dave and Lauren were heading straight for it. Beyond the brush pile was a difficult left-hand turn. Carol would have to navigate them past both obstacles. This section of the Pine was not particularly fast, and it occurred to Carol, the whole situation seemed to be happening in slow motion.

"Okay Dave, apply a little bit of rudder".

At that moment, Lauren stopped paddling. An experienced paddler knows that speed means maneuverability. To Lauren, all she knew was the brush pile was approaching and she didn't want to do anything that would cause her to hit it faster. Without power in the front of the canoe, Dave's rudder was useless and they hit a long bare log about five inches in diameter. The collision pitched the canoe's right side up so that the left side quickly filled with large quantities of water. While their canoe was still upright, neither Dave nor Lauren was still in it. Both clung to the canoe's left side as it continued toward the left hand curve.

Carol's calm voice helped Lauren and Dave remain calm. Carol quickly maneuvered her canoe along the right side of the water-filled boat and Brenda grabbed hold of the gunwales. "I'm going to try to push you over to the left bank where the water is shallow by the curve. Don't try to stand until I tell you."

The Baders and Dean's neighbors had been hanging back in case Carol needed their assistance. As they reached the gravel beach Mark Bader got out into knee-deep water to grab Dave and Lauren's water-filled boat. They stood and stumbled onto the shore, shivering in their wet clothing. Kathy helped Lauren off with her lifejacket and wet sweatshirt, ordering Dave to get his wet clothes off, too. With Lauren stripped down to her one-piece bathing suit, Kathy dressed Lauren in her own change of dry clothes. She handed Mark's dry sweatshirt to Dave.

The last two boats arrived just as Mark and Brenda rolled the water-filled boat to empty it. Almost as quickly as the canoe had filled with water, it was empty again.

Dean apologized as he stepped out of his canoe. "I'm sorry; I should have known not to start you out together on this river. Why don't we mix things up a bit?"

"Brenda," Mary said, "I understand that you are starting college next week. I'd love to hear all about it. Would you like to canoe together?"

Soon, Dave and Lauren were in dry clothes and canoes were pushing off. Mary and Brenda pushed out into the current with Kyle and Carol behind them. Brenda steered the boat tentatively at first down a long straightaway, managing to keep Mary from the overhanging branches sometimes extending from either shore. Paddling on her strong right side, her J-stroke did not have enough power on their first right turn. As they approached the curve's halfway point, the current pointed the canoe toward a pile of brush on the far bank. Several strong strokes from Mary combined with Brenda's brief stern rudder enabled them to slip by the obstacle with a yard to spare.

Carol praised her daughter's canoe handling and knew she was ready for this river. By the time they reached the white water, several hours downstream, Brenda would conquer it.

Scott and Lauren pushed off just as Mark and Kathy disappeared from sight at the end of the long straightaway. Scott resolved to take her mind off the river by engaging her in accounting shoptalk. Soon Lauren was telling him stories that only another CPA could appreciate.

Dean and Dave launched their boats right behind them. With Dave in the bow, Dean would now have the contingent's fastest boat and would take the last position for the rest of the day. "Just give me a steady stroke on the right side," he instructed. "I'll take care of everything else. If one of us gets tired, we'll switch."

Sometimes the two canoes ran side by side on long straightaways. Dave marveled at how Scott and Dean could keep their canoes at a uniform three feet apart. When Dave asked how they managed to keep their boats going so straight, Dean became a patient teacher.

Dean dropped back to the seven o'clock position behind Scott so Dave could watch Scott's technique. "Notice how his stroke is not always the same. Most of the time, he makes a straight stroke. See how the flat part of the blade comes out of the water straight back."

"Yes, I see," Dave confirmed.

Dean continued. "Scott is stronger than Lauren, so he has to compensate every few strokes. See how he sometimes twists the paddle using his upper hand. Instead of pushing water straight back, he sometimes pushes it off to the side a little as he pushes it back."

"Is that a J-stroke?" Dave asked.

"Yes, though it doesn't really look like most people write their J's. The stroke goes more back and out."

Dave watched Scott's canoe approach a right-hand turn. Scott seemed to paddle harder going into the turn. This time Scott's stroke started wide of the canoe and ended close to the stern remaining in the middle of the deepest part of the river despite the sharp right turn. He noted Lauren paddling very hard during the maneuver, but let up significantly as they entered the next straightaway. Before he could formulate a question to ask Dean, he received an explanation.

"Speed means maneuverability on a river. Stop paddling a minute and I'll demonstrate," Dean said.

Dave turned and watched him as he held his paddle hard against the side of the canoe like a rudder. They turned quickly to the left. Dean repeated the maneuver on the right-hand side pulling the canoe back to the middle of the river. He waited a few seconds until they drifted at the same speed as the river.

"Now watch what happens when I put my paddle in the water." As before, Dean put his paddle along the side of the boat as a rudder, but this time nothing happened.

"I see," said Dave, now really understanding what Dean meant.

"Scott seems to have trained Lauren about this already. If you need to rest, do it on a straight away, but always paddle hard in a turn or in white water."

"Thanks for showing me," Dave said.

An hour and a half later, they could see Mark and Kathy waving them into the lunch break on the sandy inside edge of a left-hand U bend featuring a high bank on the opposite side of the river.

"Why did we put all of the food in the last two boats?" Mark asked.

"So there would be some left for us," Scott responded.

Dean removed the bungee cord from the blue and white plastic cooler secured to his canoe's middle thwart and popped open the lid.

"Fresh fruit," he said, handing Kathy a couple of cantaloupes. Holding them chest high, she turned to carry them to the eating area.

"Nice melons," Mark remarked.

"I knew you were going to say that!" she said, shaking her head.

"Make sure you hydrate," Scott said to no one in particular as he set a two-gallon water container on some logs near the food.

Brenda and Mary were obviously having a good time, still engaged in animated conversation. "How did you do this morning?" Dean asked, giving his daughter a hug.

"She did great!" Mary answered. Brenda gave her father an account of a couple close calls, but she obviously had a very successful morning.

The canoe assignments remained the same in the afternoon, except Dean put Dave in the stern for the first hour. Dave still struggled to run a straight line, and he knew Dean often made compensating strokes to keep the canoe in the river's center. However, he felt considerably improved from the morning.

The other canoes waited for them below a bridge marking forty-five minutes left on the river. They would find white-water below this point and Dean advised Dave and Lauren to kneel on their seat cushions for the remainder of the trip to lower their center of gravity.

Dean and Dave switched back to put Dean in the stern. Dean assured him the river wouldn't look like the white water he'd seen on TV, but would still be challenging for open canoes. It provided some comfort that neither Dean nor Scott had ever tipped over in this section of river, despite having traveled it perhaps thirty times between them.

This time, all seven boats launched in quick succession. As the last two canoes paddled in tandem, the river was little different from what they had seen earlier in the day. Scott explained most of the white water would come in the last fifteen minutes. "Conserve your energy. We'll need to paddle hard in that stretch."

Dave's arms were already tired from the day's paddling. He saw Lauren with her paddle resting in her lap and Dean encouraged him to do the same. When they reached a curve, Dean said, "I'm going to need about ten hard strokes." Dave gave them to him and then they both rested. They repeated the same pattern at several other turns. In between, Dave studied the bent cedars along the riverbank and the birds that sometimes flew from the trees ahead of them. Rocks appeared more frequently now. Finally, Dean said, "Okay, give me a strong steady stroke for a while."

The sun reflected brightly off the fast-moving water as they paddled down a long westward section. Obstacles now revealed themselves in the middle of the river, not just on each side. Dave observed Scott chose a route on the shallow near side of a curve because of a huge debris pile in the deepest part of the Pine. There were few deep spots now and Dave could see the river wash up and over rocks with aluminum colored scrapes to either side of the canoe.

Ahead of him, Dave saw Scott point his canoe toward the fastest point in the river between two big rocks with water splashing over them. Well out of the water, twenty feet beyond them, sat an even larger rock. *How is this going to work?* Dave wondered, but one strong sweep of Scott's six-foot paddle and the boat pivoted twenty degrees to the right missing the third rock by a yard. Dean followed the same route and Dave suddenly realized there was a drop beyond the third rock. It was only about six inches, but he lost his balance as the boat dropped. Losing a couple of strokes, he quickly recovered and continued paddling as Dean threaded the canoe through the rocks, sometimes following Scott's route and sometimes choosing another.

Rounding a bend, Dave noticed people watching along a well-worn path on the right bank. In another two minutes, he saw the other canoes on the same shore and they beached beside them. Lauren laughed as Kathy offered her a can of beer. Mark Bader helped Scott carry the canoe away from the landing area while Carol Williams caught the other boat. As Dave got out, Lauren threw her arms around Dave and gave him a hug. He took the beer and took a long drink. Lauren's unkempt blonde hair looked wilder and more beautiful than he had ever seen it. She said, "I'd definitely do this again!"

Chapter 13

Housework Counts as Foreplay

Tuesday, September 19, 1989

The digital clock in Jack Telehowski's Taurus read 5:17 pm as he pushed his garage door opener. The sky was almost cloudless and the rusty metal Coca-Cola thermometer by the back door told him the temperature was 72 degrees. Two weeks of considerable rain left his lawn green and lush. He estimated the bent-over grass blades were five inches long. Steve promised to mow the lawn the previous weekend, but Saturday rain and Sunday teenage procrastination left the lawn uncut. With rain predicted Wednesday, Jack considered cutting the grass himself.

Marie's parking space was empty and her message on the answering machine said not to expect her home until 6:30, and to put the frozen lasagna from the laundry room freezer into the oven. Battered, with many missing paint chips, everyone now called the 35-year-old hand-me-down "the beer refrigerator," though it contained mostly pop, produce, extra milk and was seriously short of beer.

Jack returned to the kitchen with the lasagna and a can of Old Milwaukee, thinking he might as well mow the lawn since dinner would be at least an hour away.

The boys will be home from practice in twenty-minutes, but homework will be the excuse for not mowing the lawn. He set the lasagna on the counter, preheated the oven to 350 degrees and then he went into the bedroom to change.

Jack put on a tee shirt, jeans and an old pair of tennis shoes still covered with paint flecks from redoing the hallway. As he sat on the bed putting on his shoes, he noticed the unmade bed.

Marie never went without making the bed before she got the job. But today, like several other days, it sat unmade. He picked up his beer and walked into the garage to start the old Montgomery Ward lawn mower.

Jack was halfway through with the small front yard when a father from down the street dropped off Steve and Joey. He waved at the neighbor and his sons' arrival caused Jack to wonder if he had actually put the lasagna in the oven. A trip to the kitchen proved it was still on the counter.

"I guess we're having a late dinner", he said aloud, reading the cooking time on the box. *I would have been in trouble if the lasagna were still sitting there when Marie came home.*

Walking back out the garage door, he tried to remember where he put his beer. Retracing his steps, he found it on a shelf near the gas can and took a few sips before returning to the front yard to restart the mower. Jack placed the beer in a strategic location at the corner of the house out of the sun. Quickly finishing the side yard, he took a few more sips as he passed the beer.

Jack began cutting the back yard in a clockwise direction. However after the lawnmower stalled on a long grass clump from the previous pass, he reversed his course so the mower would throw the cut grass away from, rather than toward, the uncut portion of the yard. Fifty minutes later, he drank the last swallow of his now lukewarm beer and pushed the lawn mower back to the front of the house. Marie's minivan followed him into the garage.

"Is that for me?" she asked as he greeted her carrying the beer can.

"No, I'm afraid it's empty," he responded, tipping it upside down to demonstrate, "but I can get you one."

"No, I'd rather have wine."

Marie was just slipping out of her panty hose when he entered the bedroom carrying a glass of chardonnay. He enjoyed the view as she hung up her blouse, skirt and jacket. Much of her first few months take-home pay had gone to buying a new working wardrobe, including the matching white lace Victoria's Secret bra and panties that were all she was wearing. He drew her toward him and gave her a long, deep kiss.

"Why don't we have dessert first?" he asked.

"Because we have two teenage sons in the house," she responded, "both of whom are playing a computer game in the room directly below us."

"We haven't done it before dinner in four months."

"And we haven't both been home before the kids in four months either"

"What do you mean 'we?'" he asked.

"Okay, I haven't been home before the kids," she said, pushing away from him, "but they'll be hungry and I'm hungry." He noticed a tone of irritation in her voice as she pulled a casual shirt off the hanger with a little too much force. "Now, if you'll excuse me, I have dinner to cook."

While Marie put lettuce in four salad bowls, Jack went through several days' accumulated mail. She added a loaf of frozen garlic bread to the oven and groaned to no one in particular when she saw some lasagna cheese and sauce had boiled over and was now burning on the bottom of the oven.

Before she could say anything, Jack apologized for not putting a cookie sheet under the lasagna.

It was nearly 7:15 pm when they finished eating and almost 7:45 before Marie finished putting away the food and cleaning the kitchen. She hadn't been able to finish her "To Do" list the previous weekend, so she started working on the unfinished tasks. None of them were particularly time-consuming, but they were numerous and it was 10:35 before she finally climbed into the right side of their queen-sized bed with a copy of *Reader's Digest*. Jack put down his *Sports Illustrated* and moved closer to her. The feel of his body pressed up against her told her exactly what he wanted.

"Not tonight honey, I'm tired," she said gently.

"Okay," he said quietly.

Looking at him, she observed, "You look hurt."

"Well, it has been since Saturday. Did you know that we've only done it five times in the last four weeks?"

"Which is probably better than the national average," she said. "Look, honey, I have a job now. I work nine or ten hours a day, come home and make dinner, clean up, pay bills or do laundry. I just don't have any energy when ten o'clock rolls around." It was hard to argue with Marie's line of thinking, but she promised they would reconnect over the weekend.

When Marie climbed on top of him on Saturday morning, it started the hottest lovemaking session since the day she got her job. As he lay catching his breath twenty minutes later she said, "Perhaps if you did half the house work, I could generate at least half that much energy during the week."

"I think that sounds like a plan," he said.

Sunday afternoon he did the breakfast dishes after church while Marie did laundry and she surprised him by initiating sex again in the middle of the afternoon while the boys were down the street watching the Lions game with friends.

"I could get used to this," he said as she rested her head on his bare chest.

"Consider it positive reinforcement for doing housework," she said as they both dozed off.

On Monday night, Marie noticed the washing machine and dryer were both going as she entered the house from the garage. As she moved from the laundry room to the kitchen, the detergent smell gave way to cooking smells. A dining room table had a clean tablecloth with just lit candles. Jack handed her a glass of red wine and said, "Sit down, dinner will be ready in a minute. I want you to save all of your energy for later." The busy day's stress melted even before the first sip of wine. She looked around the house and heard her two sons playing a video game downstairs. As he stirred the gravy, she hugged him from behind and whispered in a low voice, "Housework by a man counts as foreplay. If we didn't have two kids in the house, I would have you right now."

Jack had cooked before, but usually just meat on the grill and rarely on a weekday. The dinner of pork chops, mashed potatoes, gravy, frozen peas and dinner rolls out of a tube was a stretch for him. He overcooked the pork chops, the potatoes were lumpy and he served the dinner rolls for dessert, but the mere effort made Marie glow with happiness. Well, perhaps the glow came from the wine. Either way, it was an extraordinary occasion in the Telehowski household.

"I think that you might be trainable," she whispered as he put the dishes in the dishwasher.

After dinner, Jack put away the food and washed the pots and pans while Marie changed out of her business clothes, helped Joey with his English and proofread the report Steve wrote for his history project. In the meantime, Jack put a load of towels in the washing machine and folded his own socks, pants and underwear. As Joey and then Steve went to bed, he told her, "Go take a nice hot bath and I'll be there in a few minutes."

As Marie soaked in the tub, she marveled at the wonderful evening. She could hear Jack enter the bedroom and recognized the sounds of him putting laundry away. She had her favorite sexy nightgown in the bathroom with her. The last time they had sex three days in a row was almost a decade before when her parents took both kids for a long weekend.

Well, he earned it and I'm going to have the energy to enjoy it too.

When he came in to brush his teeth, she hinted at the reward she had planned and said she would be out in a few minutes. After Jack left the bathroom, she toweled off and applied body powder. Marie put on the nightgown, brushed her teeth and then her hair. Giving her preparations a second thought, she added a little of his favorite perfume.

As Marie turned off the bathroom light, it took her a few seconds to become accustomed to the darkened bedroom, lit only by dimmed lights at the head of their bed. She could pick out Jack's bare chest, but not his face's features, which were in shadow. She struck a sexy pose in the bathroom door, but he did not respond. Perhaps he had not heard her enter. She posed again and cleared her throat. Still no response. She moved closer to the bed to learn why he didn't react. One close look in the dim light told her everything she needed to know. Unaccustomed to a day on the job followed by housework, Jack was asleep.

Chapter 14

The Players

Saturday, October 7, 1989

When Detroit was very young, President Jefferson appointed Augustus Woodward as the Michigan Territory's first chief justice. Woodward arrived June 30, 1805, only nineteen days after a fire destroyed most of the town of fewer than 1,500 people. As the state would not form a legislature until 1824, Governor William Hull, Woodward and two other associate Justices would possess all the territory's legislative power for another nineteen years. As Detroit was the new territory's capital, they chose to rebuild using a hub-and-spoke plan like Pierre Charles L'Enfant created for Washington, DC.

In Woodward and Hull's plan, Jefferson Avenue ran parallel to the river and Woodward Avenue became the main spoke running away from it. As often happens in politics, later administrations laid a modern grid pattern over subsequent additions, but the main spokes remain today.

In the 19th century, manufacturing and commerce made Detroit grow rapidly, and it would become one of the world's most affluent cities, claiming the title of *Paris of the West*. By 1910, many well-to-do Detroiters lived in imposing Jefferson Avenue mansions between downtown and the affluent Grosse Pointe suburbs. They entertained themselves by attending the city's many cultural events including live theater, opera and concerts.

In May that year, in an era where social activities were often segregated by gender, some women, led by Lillie

Larned, a prominent judge's wife, formed a club to provide themselves a creative outlet by producing theatrical performances one afternoon a month. The Theater Arts Club's membership list soon included many Detroit society women.

Seven months later, recognizing a good idea, their husbands formed an all men's theater group, The Players. After the club's formation in 1910, came the World War, voting rights for women, another world war, Women's Liberation, the Detroit Riots and "white flight" to the suburbs. We might guess Theater Arts and The Players would merge as a coeducational endeavor or simply disappear, yet both clubs still exist and share the same clubhouse with a third, even older, group, the Fine Arts Society of Detroit.

The men built The Players playhouse in 1925. It might catch your attention if you drive by on your daily commute. Concrete gargoyles sit at the two-story brick building's roofline. On the second floor, four pairs of tall leaded-glass doors open to nowhere but a protective railing. Above the massive double entrance doors, a six-foot interpretation of the club's logo looks out on the street. The face seems to combine a comedy mask and Bacchus, the Roman god of merriment. The ribbon above the head displays the organization's motto, "*Nunquam Renig*," bastardized Latin meaning "Never Renege". Red letters in the door's heavy lintel provide the building's only identification as "The Players."

Scott Mackenzie pulled open the thick front door. Since The Players' season runs from October to May, his last visit was the May Invitational, one of two annual events where he could bring Mary and other female guests. He discovered the Club eleven years before as a young Arthur Andersen & Co. information systems consultant working in the Renaissance Center, a mile to the southwest. He performed in his first play at the club one night after he met Mary. As a teenager, Scott performed in a few high school plays. However, the playhouse itself, as much as the opportunity to perform, attracted him to the organization. He immediately understood why longtime Player Bill Rohloff referred to it as *The Beautiful Lady*.

Scott passed through the vestibule, removing his raincoat as he entered the lobby bar. Many tuxedoed gentlemen already stood at the wooden bar choosing among three beers offered at each "Frolic." He waved as he passed through the archway painted with words from Shakespeare's **As You Like It**:

> *"All the world's a stage, and all the men and women merely players."*

On the lobby's south side, Scott mounted the broad spiral staircase leading to the second floor, hanging his raincoat on a hook along the back of the auditorium's balcony that doubled as the coatroom. Scott walked into the Founders Room just as the Twenty-Year members adjourned their annual dinner, crossing to the shelves next to the fireplace to find the white ceramic mug inscribed with his name, membership year and the club's logo.

Descending the stairs, he maneuvered his way to the bar. Two members served beer. He caught Roy Jendrzejewski's eye.

"Scott, how are you?" Roy asked.

"Thirsty!" Scott replied.

"I can help with that. What flavor?"

"Do you have a red tonight?"

"Coming right up."

As Roy filled his mug, Scott studied the oil painting above the bar featuring an attractive brunette reposing in the nude. Captured on canvas by a member decades before, the artist preserved her beauty for future generations.

Scott noted several new caricatures displayed next to the bar depicting the previous year's frolics. The lobby contained dozens selected from hundreds of past performances. Stepping through the double doors on the right side of the lobby, he entered the auditorium itself. The room always gave him the distinct feeling he had just entered the great hall of a renaissance manor. Four massive columns framed either side of the room. Five levels of round tables, six to a level, cascade to three feet below the stage. Two huge terra-cotta urns by famous Detroit sculptor Corrado Parducci flank the stage. The walls contain six Paul Honore murals on tapestry and the rafters are decorated by patterns painted by artist Thomas DiLorenzo. The building so enchanted DiLorenzo that he created a fresco above the proscenium depicting the *Seven Ages of Man* as his gift to the club.

While most amateur theater groups strictly forbid actors to consume alcohol before a performance, Players may drink before, after or even while performing onstage. When a non-Player asked why two veteran members finished off a six-pack of beer in a 35-minute performance, his host told him "because the script called for it."

A typical Frolic consists of three one-act plays, a late night dinner and then an Afterglow. Afterglows may involve almost anything: a guest appearance by a professional entertainer, singing to a guitar by a couple of members or at its best, sketch comedy written, produced, and performed by members. A character actor by preference, Scott found he had a talent for writing and became a member of one of three groups who routinely wrote their own scripts.

Scott took Michael to the club in 1986 and Michael immediately took to the concept of a once-a-month night drinking beer with the boys. The club's theatrical aspects did not interest Michael initially, but he sometimes took a role for the camaraderie. His first "young leading man" role hooked Michael on acting and he performed in four different shows the year after Laurie left him.

The club performs one full-length play a year, in November. Scott would see the play again the following weekend with Mary and Michael would play one of the main roles. Scott sat at a table with long time members Lew Davies and Bob Borsodi, making small talk until Players President Phil Gillis began with the opening announcements, which included a moment of silence for three members who died over the summer.

"Why do people you know always seem to die in threes?" Lew wondered.

"I don't know." Bob said, "but they always do."

Chapter 15

Dale Zioncheck

November 1989

Stacy D'Angelo handled non-production purchasing, such as paper, cleaning and office supplies. Purchasing people call anything that does not go directly into the product, MRO – maintenance, repairs and other. Having the president's administrative assistant purchase MRO made little sense. However, from Fairlane's earliest days, Stacy purchased MRO. For several years, purchasing manager Ken Carpenter said he should buy such items, but no one ever initiated the change since he lacked the time to buy MRO items with his ever-increasing workload buying steel, component parts and outside processing such as plating and painting.

Implementing the new computerized purchasing and receiving modules finally precipitated the change. Scott and Kathy saw the purchasing and receiving software implementation as a way to reduce paperwork. Ken saw it as a way to simplify his work and bring all of purchasing under his control.

Using the new software, engineering took responsibility for defining all production parts. Buyers created purchase orders in the computer, printed them out and mailed or faxed them to the vendor. When the goods arrived at the receiving dock, material-handling personnel entered a receiving transaction, often by scanning a barcode.

This process eliminated the need to transfer receiving documentation to accounting or to physically match it to either a purchase order or a vendor invoice. The company could pay vendors based on this computerized matching as long as both the purchasing and receiving departments followed the procedure.

As a growing company, Fairlane's purchasing workload now required two full-time people. Everyone agreed it was a good time for a buyer working for Ken to purchase both MRO and component parts which were primarily used at Fairlane's Livonia Assembly plant. John agreed with Ken's proposal to promote Stacy to buyer and find an administrative assistant to handle John's and the sales department's needs.

Stacy liked the concept of being a full-time buyer. It meant she would get her own office downstairs near Ken, a perk separating "professionals" from the clerical staff. The pay would be more, about 20 percent higher, and from her perspective, it also meant shedding the constant grunt work the sales people piled on her. Stacy was 100% for the move.

With Stacy working in purchasing, John Anderson and the Sales Department needed a new administrative assistant. Debbie was a logical person to consider for the job, so John approached Scott about offering her the position.

Many obstacles impeded selling this move to Debbie. In most companies, people would view becoming the president's administrative assistant as a promotion. Due to Debbie's college coursework, Scott already paid her more than Stacy. Stacy's reputation presented another factor. While John considered her a more-than-adequate administrative assistant, other people who worked with her, particularly Scott and Kathy, did not hold that opinion. Since the administrative assistant was also responsible for three salesmen, it was like having four bosses. Debbie didn't have to think about the offer long. She turned down the opportunity a few hours after Scott offered it.

Deciding next to look outside the company, John gave the task of finding candidates to Human Resources. Marie placed a concise, well-written advertisement in the Sunday Detroit News and by the following Wednesday collected an overwhelming 300 résumés. It took her the larger part of three days to categorize them into "A", "B" and "C" stacks. Marie delivered the "A" stack, which included nearly 25 résumés, to John's desk.

Reading résumés was John's least favorite task. He really didn't know what to look for. While he wanted to put the task off for later, he thought the Sales Department was far too busy to wait.

Scott was perplexed when John delegated screening résumés to him. As far as Scott saw it, his only connection to choosing the administrative assistant was that Marie, the Human Resources manager, reported to him. Still, he thrived on variety and welcomed the break from the project on his desk. Realizing the sales people would have a strong opinion about candidate selection, he went upstairs for their input.

Arriving upstairs only minutes after the weekly sales meeting ended, Scott found Bud and Mike in Ray's office listening to him tell a dirty joke. Waiting for Ray to finish, Scott said, "That's one of my favorites."

"You've heard it?" Ray asked. Scott nodded.

"Yeah, me too," Michael added, "but it's still good."

Scott found it was easy to get Michael, Ray and Bud involved at narrowing down the interview list. Within an hour, they had selected five names from the "A" list for Marie to screen further. Phone interviews allowed her to eliminate two more candidates and she invited the three who passed this hurdle for in-depth office interviews. She rank prioritized these three and setup an interview for candidate #1 with John.

The following Tuesday, after a relatively short half-hour interview he came into Marie's office and said, "She'll do."

"Do you want to interview the other candidates?" she asked.

"No," he said "She'll do" and that was that.

"The following Monday, Dale Zioncheck, 42, arrived. She was 5'9" but looked as if she weighed only 120 lbs. wearing a mid-calf length black and white knit dress. Her hair, which she wore up, was obviously naturally blonde. Ken saw her sitting in the lobby awaiting Marie's arrival as he walked in the front door at 7:50 a.m. Soon Ken was brewing her a pot of decaf in the break room. When Marie arrived, Joan Robbins informed her that Ken had gone toward the break room with the new hire. Marie tracked them down just as Ken was pouring the coffee into Dale's mug. She guessed that Ken wouldn't be the only man who would go out of his way to welcome the new hire.

It pleased Stacy to have a major role in orienting the new administrative assistant. It did not please her to find her new buyer job also included an abbreviated two-week orientation process. After all, she handled MRO purchasing for most of the last ten years. It surprised her even more to learn the training's primary purpose was to learn how to use the purchasing software that Kathy and Scott would teach her. Kathy also scheduled Ken to attend the sessions since he was also just learning the software himself.

As usual, Dale's thirty-day orientation plan began with Marie in Human Resources. Computer orientation with

Kathy came next followed by a joint session with Dave and Scott that involved discussing the routine flow of sales expense reports and information flow between sales and accounting.

Later that day, as Dave and Scott talked about Livonia plant budgets in Dave's office, Marie stuck her head in and asked, "What did you think?"

"Close the door," Scott said. Marie did and he continued; "I thought she seemed very smart, but also very sad. Did you think she seemed sad?" he asked, turning to Dave.

"Yes, now that you mention it. Sad is a good description. But maybe it was first day tension."

"No, I think that she's having a tough time in her life," Marie said. "She's a single mom with two teenage daughters. Her last job was in California and she moved back to Michigan to be near her parents. She showed me a picture of her two daughters and they didn't look much like each other. I suspect this may not have been her first divorce."

It pleased Marie to know that both Scott and Dave thought Dale was a good hire. Stacy moved into the office next to Ken's a week later and began her own orientation.

While Kathy and Marie bonded instantly, Kathy and Stacy had never really hit it off, despite working together for nearly four years. The first purchasing software training session would include Stacy but not Ken, since his training began before John agreed to move Stacy to Purchasing. A few minutes after the session ended, Kathy walked into Scott's office.

"What year is it?" she asked.

Wondering if Kathy was asking a trick question, he looked at his wall calendar and then examined his pocket appointment book. Seeing that the numbers agreed, he finally gave an answer in keeping with the question's off-the-wall nature. "In the Judeo-Christian world I'm pretty sure it's 1989."

"That's what I thought too," she said, "but one of our co-workers seems to think it's 1977."

Realizing what Kathy must have been doing that morning, he understood her irritation.

"Would that co-worker happen to be Stacy D'Angelo?" Scott asked.

"How did you figure that out?" Kathy said sarcastically.

"She's the only person in the company who ever used White-Out on a computer screen."

They both knew Ray started this rumor as a joke, but since people repeated it so many times, the story was now a well-known company legend. Kathy didn't laugh at Scott's attempt at humor.

"Get this. She thinks using a computer isn't a "professional" thing to do. If she needs data entered, she expects a clerical person to do it!"

"Did she have any particular clerical person in mind?"

"That wasn't clear, but I suspect she would try to give it to Dale or someone in accounting."

Only three office personnel didn't have a computer on their desk: John Anderson, Bud Pierce, and Ray Peltier who at 48, 64 and 62 were among the oldest people in the company. After a lengthy recounting of Kathy's session with Stacy, they decided to reevaluate the situation after Scott's Excel tutoring sessions with her.

Several others at Fairlane were proficient Excel users, principally Dave and Debbie. However, Scott taught the sessions himself because he liked to teach and was good at it. He periodically held spreadsheet training sessions for anyone who wanted to attend. As a result, virtually all of the office, with the exception of John, Bud, Ray and Stacy, could do at least the basics.

Scott had no chance to evaluate Stacy's computer skills that week because she made an excuse to cancel their session. Since he had several full-day continuing education seminars the following week, Stacy's Excel lesson would have to wait. She continued to meet with Kathy, about the purchasing software, but required twice the training time as Ken. In the meantime, Stacy continued to purchase MRO items via typed purchase orders and Ken continued to purchase component parts.

Back in the office the next Friday, Scott joined Ken and the three salespeople for lunch at a restaurant on Fairlane Mall's perimeter drive. Michael quickly steered the discussion to the Sales Department's most important topic of the day. "I'm afraid Ray didn't get anything done all week."

"Too many distractions upstairs," Ray said. "I can't decide whether I should stare at her legs, ass, face or tits."

"I recommend looking at her eyes," Scott said. "Staring at other parts of a woman's body can lead to a sexual harassment charge. I think for the first offense, Marie would probably send you to a chauvinist rehabilitation program."

"That step may be closer than you think," Michael countered. "Ray can't help staring at Marie's tits either."

"Tell the truth guys," Ray said. "Have you ever seen a woman over forty years old who looked that good? I think

I've seen Dale somewhere before. Maybe on TV or in a magazine."

"If she looks familiar to Ray," Ken quipped, "it's probably because she used to be a stripper."

Scott interjected; "Well, she looks familiar to me, too; but, since she has lived in California for twenty years, I don't think you saw her in a strip joint. But, you know guys, this is one of our co-workers we're talking about. This is almost 1990 and any inappropriate references in a business setting regarding her appearance could get us, as well as the company, in a lot of trouble."

"So you're saying we can only talk about her at lunch?" Michael cracked.

"Yes," Scott replied hesitantly, as if he were not 100 percent sure that this was okay either.

"The difference between you two," Ken observed, "is that Scott has a photographic memory and Ray has a pornographic memory." They all laughed.

Dale didn't look familiar to anyone other than Scott and Ray, and Scott tried to change the subject; "To the really important business issue: is she an improvement over Stacy?"

The question stirred Bud from his role as a quiet observer. "My God, Scott, she actually knows how to use a computer. Stacy just threw all her files in one directory and had no labeling system. Sometimes she would take forever to find a letter she typed last week. Dale set up separate directories for every customer and then sub-directories for every buyer. I can't believe we got Purchasing to take Stacy off our hands. I feel like we're the winners here."

"Gee, you make me feel like I just bought a white elephant," Ken said.

"I'm sure Stacy will be a fine buyer," Bud said. "But she was a lousy secretary."

"Administrative assistant," Scott corrected him.

"OK, Stacy was a lousy administrative assistant," Bud said. "She's a really nice person, but I'm glad Dale is working with us now."

When the time came for her Excel training with Scott, Stacy asked to reschedule because she left her glasses at home and wouldn't be able to see the screen without them. Constantly deferring training was becoming a problem and Scott talked to Ken about it. Now, Kathy was not the only person getting impatient with Stacy.

That Saturday, Scott thinned out his clothes closet while Mary accompanied their daughters to a birthday party at Chuck E. Cheese. As he worked, his eyes fell on several boxes he had not opened since he and Mary moved in together. Getting a damp cloth to wipe the dust off the covers, he opened the first box to find old textbooks, a few term papers and some college mementos. Underneath them were at least three dozen vintage issues of Playboy. On a hunch, he started thumbing through the centerfolds. He found what he was looking for in an issue dated 1973. With her hair up, wearing high heels and nothing else was an attractive blonde twisted to look at the camera exposing her bare bottom and a perfect left breast. He thumbed through the entire layout, carefully examining the face and every other part of her anatomy. The first name matched, but the last name was different.

"Ray wouldn't believe this," Scott thought. He set the issue aside, and returned the boxes to their place in the back of the closet. As he continued thinning out old clothes, he realized he couldn't share what he found. As he looked at the beautiful young girl, he said to himself, *OK, you're probably having a very hard time right now. This would undoubtedly embarrass you and distract everybody if word got out. I'll keep your secret.*

Chapter 16

The Christmas Party

Saturday, December 9, 1989

"What am I supposed to wear to this thing?" Jack asked Marie as she came into the bedroom, freshly showered and wrapped in a towel.

"Kathy says nice casual," Marie said as she disappeared into their walk-in closet. "I'm wearing black slacks and my red blouse."

Jack rummaged through his dresser.

"Wear something Christmassy," Marie added.

"I don't have anything Christmassy," he responded.

As she slipped on her bra and panties, she suspected he would need some guidance and emerged from the closet carrying a pair of khaki slacks and a white shirt.

"Wear these with your green sweater."

She knew Jack was not particularly fond of the sweater, but he found it in his bottom drawer and put on what she had chosen."

For some reason, going to the company Christmas party at John and Barbara Anderson's house made Marie apprehensive. Most office and management personnel would be there with their dates or spouses. She had met Barbara only once before when she came to have lunch with John. Slim, fit and well dressed, she fit the image of a CEO's wife. Marie was not sure they would have anything in common to talk about. Even though Franklin was only 20 miles away, Marie had rarely been to any of Detroit's affluent northwest suburbs and had never been to Franklin.

As Jack drove north on Telegraph Road, the streets were clear and dry with no snow in the immediate forecast.

Meanwhile, in Farmington Hills, Lauren said, "Let's go over names," as she got into Dave's car. "I remember most of the people from the canoe trip. Your boss is Scott, the CFO and his wife is Mary. Dean is the Engineering VP and his wife is Carol. Kathy handles IT. What was her husband's name?"

"Mark, Mark Bader. He was Scott's roommate in college."

"Who else should I know?"

"Well, you haven't met anybody else, but our hosts are John and Barbara Anderson. I haven't met Barbara either. Don't worry about anyone else; I'll introduce you when we get there. Scott said that there were name tags last year because a lot of people don't know the spouses."

Spouses? Dave couldn't believe he had just used the term "spouses" to refer to all of the non-Fairlane guests, including his girlfriend. Lauren didn't say anything about his choice of words, but seemed to have a happy, satisfied look on her face as she pulled back the faux fur hood on her white winter jacket.

No one was as nervous about the party as Barbara Anderson. Eight years before when they had only a dozen guests, she fretted about the details so much that John insisted she hire a caterer the following year. Since she feared forgetting names, she provided nametags on a table near the front door and assigned Michael the job of taking pictures each year so that she could review faces with John before the next year's party.

Still, the differences between Barbara and her husband's employees made her the most uneasy. The Detroit Metro area was so vast that someone from the Northwest Suburbs might not know the communities in the Southern suburbs. For the most part, they lived in different kinds of neighborhoods, shopped in different stores and led different lives. Barbara hoped she wouldn't be too much of an embarrassment for her husband and resolved to spend time mingling with people she didn't already know.

It was a big party. After the buffet dinner, Michael overheard some of the women talking about a musical that had just finished its Detroit production. One thing, or perhaps one drink, led to another and soon Barbara was playing show tunes on her grand piano while a small crowd sang along. She had never had such fun at her own Christmas party.

Shortly after midnight, Jack and Marie left the Anderson's front door. "I'm glad you're driving," Jack said as he got into the passenger side of his Taurus.

"How many did you have?" Marie asked

"Four, I think, but that's double what I usually have. Ken and Ray were a riot. I hardly talked to anyone else all evening. It looked like you were having a great time. Who were you singing with at the piano?"

"Michael Anderson, Barbara Anderson, Mary Mackenzie and Carol Williams."

"All the C-Suite spouses. Good for you."

"They were very nice ladies, and they were all about my age. I wish we lived closer, I'd love to see them all more often."

"Well, we can't afford to live closer," Jack said, dashing Marie's fantasy.

"I know. But it was nice to be able to live in their world for at least one evening."

As their last guests walked out the door, Barbara remarked to John, "You have some great people working for you. We're really fortunate."

Chapter 17

Another Friday

Friday December 16, 1989

After a week of temperatures fluctuating between 5 and 28 degrees, the morning Detroit Free Press said there was a 70 percent chance of one to two inches of snow and a white Christmas looked likely. Debbie long ago replaced her short summer dresses with turtleneck sweaters. Kathy wore a fur-lined bomber hat and Michael wore his timeless camel overcoat

With Barbara Anderson's younger daughter now a college freshman, attending and supporting her children's activities ended abruptly. Her Junior League meetings and volunteer activities continued, but having an empty nest left a void in her life. She needed a new hobby.

On Wednesday morning, Barbara drove just over two miles to play doubles tennis with some girlfriends. At 11 a.m. on Friday, she took lessons and sometimes, on Sunday morning, she played singles with John.

Working out three or more times a week gave Barbara a "wife of a successful man" look. She had slender arms and legs, a thin waist and a flat stomach. She had her hair done weekly and purchased most of her clothes at Bonwit Teller or Saks Fifth Avenue at upscale Somerset Mall in Troy or at fashionable shops in Birmingham. Sure, Barbara had a couple of wrinkles, but most women her age had a lot more.

Leaving the club, Barbara drove to their Franklin home in less than five minutes. Thirty years before, Franklin was little more than a few buildings clustered around the intersection of two Oakland County "mile roads." Now it contained the fine homes of powerful executives and politicians.

Franklin Village covers just less than three square miles but manages to avoid any look of suburbia. Overall, the village remains an almost rural oasis amid metro Detroit's suburban sprawl.

John and Barbara Anderson owned a tastefully elegant Franklin home. Set on an irregularly shaped lot of two full acres, stately mature oak trees dotted the yard. Their neighbors' homes sat far enough away that there was plenty of privacy, even without pulling the curtains. The house was field stone and gray clapboard with expansive windows. While only twelve years old, the Anderson's four bedroom, three-and-a-half bath home looked like a timeless classic.

Barbara parked her beige Lincoln Mark VII in the garage, entering the house just two steps from her driver's side door. She left the large double garage door open as she closed the mudroom door and hung up her casual winter coat. Opening the auxiliary refrigerator near the garage door, she extracted a Diet Pepsi and flipped her tennis visor onto a peg. Passing the kitchen counter, she broke off a perfectly ripe banana, peeling it and taking a bite as she walked the length of the house to the master suite.

Leaving the bedroom door open, she walked into the master bath, removed her sweaty sleeveless tennis top and tossed it into the laundry hamper under the counter. Returning to the bedroom, she removed her shoes and tennis footies, carefully setting the shoes on a shoe shelf in her walk-in closet before returning to the master bath.

Removing the rest of her clothes, Barbara stood in front of the mirror, looking at the image of her own naked body.

Running her hands over her stomach, she thought *nearly flat, but I could be firmer. I could use some sit-ups.* However, she hated sit-ups and would probably not follow up on this idea.

Turning on the shower, Barbara washed down the rest of the banana with the Diet Pepsi while waiting for the water to warm. A few seconds later, she was rubbing shampoo into her short brown hair and lathering her body to remove the workout sweat. She rinsed her hair and shaved her underarms and bikini line. Turning off the water, she reached for the plush white towel outside the shower door and dried herself before putting on a thick white robe.

Standing in front on the steamy mirror, Barbara wiped a spot clear with a hand towel before drying her hair with the blow dryer. Over the noisy hair dryer, she didn't hear a car pull into the garage, the garage door close, the mudroom door open and close or the footsteps crossing the tile in front of the living room fireplace. In fact, she first realized she was not alone when she heard the bedroom door close a millisecond after she turned off the hair dryer.

"Is that you?" she asked. The familiar voice replied, "Yes, it is" and a minute later, they were embracing at the foot of the bed, their lips locked in a long, deep kiss. Coming up for air, Barbara pulled the short-sleeve sports shirt off her 36-year-old tennis pro, as he slipped the white robe from her shoulders and let it fall to the floor. A minute later, they were both naked on the bed and he was deep inside her as he usually was early on a Friday afternoon. Ten minutes later and exhausted, she fell asleep with her head on his shoulder.

This particular Friday, Barbara was not the only member of the Anderson family enjoying "afternoon delight". At that very moment, her young brother-in-law was not far from the company's offices in a hotel with a married woman. Michael had only been with one other married woman before, a graduate teaching assistant (TA) for a class he took his last semester at Michigan State. She invited herself to the drinking party Michael and his friends planned after their final, final exam. The exam finished at 10:30 a.m. By 11 a.m., his case study group was at the bar and by 2 p.m., Michael and the TA were back at Michael's apartment engaged in hot sweaty sex. Two naps and three hours later she was gone from his life forever, having given him an unforgettable ending to his four years in East Lansing.

The woman this afternoon was a different story. Generally, Michael made it a policy never to flirt with a married woman. The potential for complications seemed too great. Truthfully, he avoided flirting with her, but when she flirted with him, somehow his lack of reciprocation only made her more aggressive. A few months before she managed to get herself very alone with him and in the heat of the moment he had sex with her. It happened three more times since then, but he decided this was going to be the last time. Since she insisted on spending the afternoon "fucking his brains out" he decided to let her and break up with her gently sometime in the future.

That moment might still be a couple of weeks away. Right now, she stood in front of him completely nude with perky nipples on firm white breasts. As he admired her figure, she unbuttoned his shirt, then his pants and in a few minutes, they would unite in the queen-sized bed.

Back at Fairlane Tool and Manufacturing, a minor crisis occupied Scott Mackenzie and he could not find Michael Anderson. The crisis involved Michael's mother, Betty.

John Anderson usually had lunch with their mother at noon on Fridays. Sometimes he took her to lunch, but most of the time they just ate at her kitchen table. Since Betty Anderson lived in Dearborn Heights, not far from the company, John could usually have lunch with her and be back to the office in no more than an hour and a half.

John thought he might not visit his mother today because he, Michael and two of his sisters had a big birthday dinner for her just that past Sunday. He called mid-morning to discuss lunch and her voice alarmed him as they talked on the phone. She sounded groggy, disoriented and didn't make much sense when she talked. Fifteen minutes later, he was at her door and soon they were at the Oakwood Hospital emergency room.

John tried to call Barbara from the pay phone in the waiting room, but remembered she had a weekly tennis lesson when the answering machine picked up. He left no message, but used his remaining change to call Michael at the office. Joan Robbins told him Michael left for the afternoon. Since it was lunch hour for most of the office staff, he asked Joan to transfer him to Scott who was one of the few people in the office.

The protocol for a manager signing out was to notify Joan of their destination, but Michael left no indication of where he was going. By now, it was nearly half-past noon and Scott found all three sales people's offices completely dark. Michael's "Day-Timer" was not on his desk and the large calendar pad on Dale's desk that sometimes showed where her four charges would be was also completely blank for the day. Scott phoned both the Fairlane Club's formal and casual dining areas, but Michael was not there. Scott knew there was a car phone mounted on the console of

Michael's Mercury and quickly found the number on Dale's Rolodex. Likewise, Michael was not in his car.

With no clue to discovering Michael's whereabouts, he called John back at the pay phone. By this time, John realized there was nothing anybody else could do. He said not to put any more effort into finding Michael, noting that he would call his sisters later that afternoon when he knew more.

Three hours after John's initial phone call, his mother was sleeping and in stable condition. Since John was hungry and not in the mood to return to work, he headed home having asked Scott to cancel his 2 p.m. planning meeting with Jimmy.

John was unaccustomed to how quickly the Southfield Freeway moved early in the afternoon and reached Franklin quickly. As he approached his driveway, he saw a car leaving his driveway and his garage door closing. Looking at the other car's driver, he recognized the tennis pro as their cars passed. He found Barbara standing at the kitchen counter eating a cup of yogurt dressed in only the white robe. The look on her face confirmed exactly what John instantly realized as he saw the car, beginning a tear-filled exchange lasting well into the evening.

Second only to the day his father died, John would later think of it as the worst day of his life.

Chapter 18

Out of Touch

Friday, January 26, 1990

Each U.S. domestic automaker shuts down production for a week or more between Christmas and New Year and another two weeks each summer. Fairlane always observed a similar Christmas shutdown and then worked a reduced schedule for the three weeks when Ford and Chrysler's summer shutdowns overlapped. This time, Fairlane's Christmas shutdown had lasted ten days.

Christmas was now a month ago and while Michigan should have been in the deepest part of winter, temperatures had been above average since December 29th, the longest stretch of above-average temperatures since 1959. At 36 degrees, it wasn't a bad January day.

No one noticed yet, but John Anderson was spending significantly fewer hours in the office. His mother's medical problem proved not to be a stroke and even though she was reasonably back to normal, he and his sisters convinced her to move to a retirement community. Betty Anderson now lived conveniently close to her oldest daughter, who was the second of her five children, 50 miles west in Chelsea.

The combination of his marital problems and his mother's issues left John unable to concentrate on work. He cancelled Barbara's Franklin Racket Club membership, forcing her to make the 25 minute drive to the Fairlane Club to play tennis. She was mortified and remorseful when John discovered her afternoon adventures. On Monday mornings, they went to marriage counseling and twice a week Barbara had lunch with her husband at the Fairlane Club sports bar after her workout.

Just before lunchtime on Friday, John told his new administrative assistant he was leaving in an hour to go to Florida for two weeks. Only two months into her new job, Dale managed to hide her surprise that her new boss would take off for two weeks without giving her any notice.

"If a problem comes up that needs immediate attention, give it to Mack if it involves operations, Dean if it involves engineering or quality, Bud if it involves sales and let Scott figure out anything else." He gave Dale an emergency phone number, noting that they were staying in a rented condo, not a hotel, so there probably wasn't an answering machine. "If anyone doesn't get through to me on the first try, tell them to try again later."

John was gone before Dale discovered that none of the people John listed knew his plans either. Scott found the number's 813 area code covered western Florida, noting that sometimes the Anderson's vacationed near Sarasota where many of their Franklin neighbors wintered.

Monday, January 29, 1990

Dave saw Debbie sitting at the receptionist's desk as he returned from a long weekend. He and Lauren had taken Friday afternoon off to go "Up North", a vaguely defined area that all Michiganders understand to be anywhere above the lower half of "the mitten".

"It looks like you got some sun," she remarked, looking at his obviously sunburned face.

"Yeah, a bit," he responded. "Lauren and I went cross country skiing. It never occurred to me to wear sunscreen."

"Now, you know. Hey, you missed all the excitement when you were gone on Friday."

"Why, what's going on?"

"Ken fired Stacey, Joan is going to purchasing and Marie is looking for a new receptionist."

"Really!" Dave said. "What happened?"

"I don't know the details, but I think it had to do with an inventory problem. Ask Kathy or Marie."

Dave turned and saw the two women talking in Marie's office. He knocked on Marie's open door. They welcomed him in and Kathy asked about his weekend. After giving a brief summary, he asked about Stacey.

"Shut the door," Marie said. "Do you want to begin?" she asked Kathy.

"She obviously wasn't getting it," Kathy said. "She skipped half her computer training sessions but finally started using the purchasing system when Ken forced her. Last week Ken discovered she purchased $60,000 of an expensive split-pin rivet that the computer clearly showed has zero future demand on a part whose production ended three weeks ago. She frustrated Ken, she frustrated me and she frustrated Scott. So, she's gone."

Monday, February 12, 1990

Since John had little conversation with his two vice presidents in two months, nothing seemed unusual when he asked them both to lunch on the Monday he returned.

As John and Dean appeared at Scott's door at 11:45 a.m., John remarked. "Let's go to the Fairlane Club. I haven't eaten in the main dining room in a long time. Scott noticed that when John moved the white markers on the In/Out board by the reception desk, he set the "will return" time to 2:00 p.m.

The Fairlane Club's main dining room was well populated as the hostess seated them at a square table in the middle of the room. Soon, the waiter poured them each a Heineken into a tall pilsner glass as they reviewed the menu. After ordering, John shared what was on his mind. "Sitting at the pool gave me an opportunity to think about the next few years. In a couple of years, we're going to be a big company. None of us has experience running an operation of $70 million, particularly me. I've been thinking that soon we are going to need to hire an Operations VP."

Neither Dean nor Scott had an issue with John's concept. If they hired such a person, John could focus more on sales and the person they hired would focus on manufacturing. The surprise came when John said he wanted to hire someone right now.

"While I was in Florida, I met a guy who was, until recently, a VP at Kelsey-Hayes. He has a lot of experience running big manufacturing plants."

John pulled two copies of a résumé from his suit pocket and handed one each to Dean and Scott. Dean ticked off the résumé's most important points as Scott read silently while buttering and consuming a dinner roll.

"BS in Civil Engineering from West Virginia. ROTC with four years in the US Army, Captain with one in Vietnam. He lives in Ann Arbor, has an MBA from Eastern and work experience at six different manufacturing companies including two of our major competitors. I think we should interview him."

"I already have," John said. Then added hastily, "but, of course, I want you guys to interview him too."

Chapter 19

Angus McGrath

Wednesday, February 14, 1990

Two days later, Angus McGrath sat in Scott's guest chair after having spent somewhat less than an hour with Dean Williams.

Scott had not expected such a big man. He judged McGrath to be 6'3" and 250 pounds, bigger than John, but not quite as large as Mack. His hair was thinning on both sides of his forehead but not in the middle, where he had short graying dark brown hair. His complexion was uneven and he was neither handsome nor pleasant-looking. Scott opened with one of his usual questions.

"Where are you from?"

McGrath did not seem to welcome the question. "Morgantown, West Virginia, or at least close to it. My family had a farm way out of town."

"What did you grow?"

"Some corn, hay and we had some dairy cattle and pigs."

As his story unfolded, Scott learned that, despite his enormous size, McGrath had never played sports in either high school or college, his father requiring him to take care of the farm animals every afternoon. He hated farm living, did not seem to care for "his old man" and attended local West Virginia University on an ROTC scholarship as a way of escaping farm life, graduating at the Vietnam War's height.

McGrath soon turned around the line of questioning. Scott's affluent northern suburbs background could not have been more different than McGrath's. Scott was tennis team captain at an elite high school, had two degrees from the University of Michigan, was his fraternity's president and spent five years as an information systems consultant with a "Big Eight" accounting firm. Rather than impress McGrath, Scott's résumé seemed to annoy him.

The interview was not going well. McGrath asked some questions about the company's finances.

"What's our market capitalization?"

Scott thought it was an oddly worded question. A public company's market capitalization is its current share price times the number of shares outstanding. However, since Fairlane was not a public company, financial people would use the term market value or fair market value in this situation. It appeared McGrath just threw out a buzzword he did not really understand. Scott did not correct him and gave a number reflecting the valuation from the current shareholder's buy-sell agreement.

Before Scott could turn the conversation back to the candidate and how he might fit in at Fairlane, the big man looked at his watch and said, "John and I were planning to have an early lunch. Thanks for taking the time to meet with me." McGrath rose, and then he was out of Scott's door.

When John returned from lunch with McGrath mid-afternoon, he asked Dean and Scott to come to his office.

"Both of you had some time with him. What do you think of Bull?"

"Bull?" Scott asked.

"Yes, he doesn't like the name Angus. He prefers Bull."

Dean went first. "He has a pretty good résumé and good work experience for what we do. I think we ought to hire him."

John turned to Scott. "What do you think?"

"I don't know what it is about him, but I don't think he would fit into our culture. The questions he asked weren't very good. His degrees aren't from top tier schools. Whatever he is going to cost us would be at least twenty to thirty percent of this year's profits. Maybe we need someone in this position in the future, but I don't think we need someone right now and I don't think this is the guy."

John responded, "Can you be more specific about what you didn't like about Bull?"

"I'm not sure I can. I can't pinpoint what it is, but I just don't think he would fit in with our culture."

The three of them talked about Bull McGrath for another ten minutes. John had now spent a total of almost eight hours with McGrath. Scott and John had spent barely an hour between them. It never occurred to anyone that Dean and Scott had inadequate time with the candidate and neither VP had any hint John wanted someone else to run the company so that he could devote more time to repairing his damaged marriage.

John felt lucky to find someone with experience running a much bigger operation. He felt confident that Bull McGrath was just the person he needed. John and Scott did not always agree. At just 37 years old, sometimes the things Scott said sounded youthful and naive. Was Scott jealous that John was about to hire another senior executive? Sure, sometimes John regretted not doing things that Scott advised, but this time, John was sure he was right.

Finally, John said, "Well, the vote is two to one. I guess we hire him." Bud and Ray, Fairlane's senior salespeople, would later call it the worst human resources decision either of them had ever observed in their long careers.

Chapter 20

McGrath's Orientation

Monday, February 19, 1990

As human resources manager, Marie's responsibilities included making sure all new employees had a 30-Day Plan. Thus, she asked John how he planned to orient Angus McGrath. For manufacturing employees, the company used a standard structured plan that Jimmy developed. However, for a manager, each person's immediate supervisor created the plan based on the situation's specific needs.

While John introduced the 30-Day Plan concept after attending a president's roundtable a decade before, he rarely developed one himself. A few hours after Marie's inquiry, John dropped off a few hand-written notes, suggesting she talk with Dean and Scott about their ideas and work it into a specific schedule.

A day and a half later, Marie presented their collective ideas to John on a spreadsheet. He made a few minor changes and thus established the plan for McGrath's first four weeks at Fairlane. Marie provided the finalized plan to everyone McGrath would meet with as well as two copies to John - one for him and one for McGrath.

In announcing McGrath's hiring to his management team, John referred to the date two weeks hence when he would start as "B-Day". Jimmy didn't quite hear him properly and thought he said "P-Day". It got a good laugh from everyone but John himself and the name stuck.

With other things on his mind, it did not occur to John to discuss the 30-Day Plan concept with McGrath or even copy him on the schedule in advance. Thus, John surprised

McGrath when he told him people who were, for the most part, one or two levels below him on the organizational chart would tutor him about the company for the first four weeks. Still, being new, McGrath decided not to try to change this practice on his very first day.

As the second name on the schedule, McGrath surprised Marie when he asked her to come to his office instead of coming to hers where she had all the human resources forms and supplies readily available. She shook her head about this unusual venue but packed up the forms and documents she had set aside and walked up the north stairs to McGrath's office, which had formerly been a small conference room across the reception area from John.

Marie tried to start the meeting by describing the company's normal orientation process. McGrath quickly shut her off, explaining that John had already discussed the process with him. Assuming that he knew the process included getting to know each other; Marie switched gears to ask him to tell her about himself. She got nothing that she didn't already know from the résumé and he quickly turned the conversation toward the documents she brought.

Marie's stack was several inches thick including payroll withholding forms, benefit forms, benefit booklets, the employee handbook and a form the company's lawyer required confirming that each new team member had read the employee handbook.

"Your 30-Day Plan gives you plenty of time to do this today. Expect it will take about 90 minutes to read the employee manual and another hour to fill out all the forms."

When she got to the lawyer's form, McGrath just rolled his eyes. Marie sensed that McGrath couldn't wait to get her out of his office and thus ended her short introduction to the company's new COO.

An hour later, as McGrath signed the very last form, he saw it was time for the next 30-Day Plan meeting. He looked down his phone list and asked Scott Mackenzie to come upstairs. Scott resisted the suggestion, pointing out they would have far better access to information in accounting than in McGrath's almost bare office. Scott noticed McGrath's face appeared flushed when he arrived and seemed to have a look of contempt. Scott ignored the look and guided the COO to a seat next to him at the table that served as his deck.

"Welcome aboard," Scott said. "Let's walk you through the various reports you'll get and how to interpret them. I'll start with financial reports; then, we'll talk about operating reports."

The cover sheet on the monthly financial package showed key operating statistics, significant budget variances and discussed the previous month's results. Behind that was a summarized income statement followed by a semi-detailed version of the same information running six pages. Afterwards, Scott showed a detailed statement for every department reporting to McGrath in a monthly and year-to-date actual to budget format.

"Do you have a quarterly version of these reports?" McGrath asked.

"No," Scott replied. "We're not a public company and don't have any reason to create a quarterly report."

"How about for the board of directors?" McGrath asked.

"While our board meets once a quarter," Scott responded, "they normally meet one month before the quarter ends, so a quarterly report would reflect old data."

"Can you prepare ME a quarterly financial report?" McGrath asked.

"Yes, if that's what you'd like," Scott said. "We charge system change requests to the department requesting it. I'll get you an estimate of how much the change would cost."

McGrath did not like the concept of having the new report come out of his budget, but the conversation moved on to the company's balance sheet. McGrath seemed to study the balance sheet with great interest. "Can you give this to me in a quarterly format as well?"

Scott didn't quite know how to respond to the question. Since a balance sheet represents a company's financial position at a particular point in time, there is no such thing as a quarterly balance sheet. Scott would not consider this a dumb question from someone who had no financial education or experience. However, McGrath's résumé listed an MBA from Eastern Michigan University and experience as a public company vice president. Any MBA program requires at least one accounting class. Now, McGrath obviously just pretended to have a deep understanding of the balance sheet before him. Had he lied on his résumé, or did he just not pay attention in class?

After a moment, which he hoped would look like a deep and thoughtful consideration of McGrath's request, Scott wrote a note on a pad of white lined paper and said, "I'll see what I can come up with."

Their focus now turned to the Manufacturing Productivity Report comparing actual production with the standard for each production run for every product. To Scott's relief, McGrath really seemed to understand the report this time and seemed to consider it very valuable information. Scott, Kathy and Jimmy jointly designed the report, consolidating no less than four standard reports from their software package.

Next McGrath asked, "What about product profitability reports? What reports do we routinely produce and what can I get?"

"What kind of information would you like?" Scott asked.

"I want to know the actual costs of everything we produce and how much money we make or lose on each product," McGrath responded.

"You mean actual direct costs?"

"No, I mean actual total costs," McGrath replied.

Again, Scott didn't quite know how to react. Since indirect costs are difficult to trace to a specific product and a third or more of all costs are indirect at most companies, someone who actually understood what they were talking about would not use the terms "total" and "actual" in the same sentence.

Scott measured his response carefully. "If you could tell me how you plan to use the information it would help me understand how to format the report for you."

Despite Scott's attempt to be polite and tactful, McGrath reacted as if the question irritated him and his face flushed again. "I'm going to use it to focus on improving profitability on products we're losing money on."

In other industries, management might seek to discover money-losing products and simply discontinue them. However, an auto supplier cannot discontinue a part because most parts are single-sourced and their customers need those parts to make cars. Thus, it is not possible to improve profitability by eliminating existing products. It was also not possible to improve profitability by raising price since customer contractual arrangements define how price can go up, or more often down, over a product's life.

Realizing now that McGrath might have little idea what he was talking about when it came to anything financial, Scott said; "We have several different types of cost reports available. Why don't I bring them up to your office this afternoon and we can figure out which one will work best for you."

Two hours later, Scott and Kathy sat 90 degrees to each other at the Dearborn Big Boy restaurant. As the waitress took their food orders to the kitchen, Kathy said, "We both just spent an hour with our new COO. What did you think of him?"

"Well," he hesitated as he looked for the words to describe his thoughts, "He certainly hasn't made a very favorable impression on me so far."

"Hello, Scott, this is Kathy. You can tell me what you really think."

"Well, maybe it's a guy thing. You know how we aren't very good at expressing our feelings. Maybe you should go first."

"I think he's an idiot."

"So you're neutral about him," Scott quipped, taking a sip of ice water from the red plastic glass in front of him.

"First of all, he pulls this crap where he wants me to come up to his office to give him his systems orientation. So, I play along and go to his office and I begin by showing him how to log in. I'm guessing he never used a computer before because he didn't even know how to turn it on. He was the worst typist I've ever seen.

"Two fingers?" Scott asked.

"Worse. One finger."

"So when he gets to two fingers he'll be twice as good."

The situation frustrated Kathy. "How can you joke about this? The guy's an asshole."

"But unfortunately," Scott said grimly "he's our asshole now."

Chapter 21

Excellence is Standard

Monday, February 26, 1990

In the first week, Angus McGrath obligingly followed the 30-Day Plan. So far, he had fifteen separate one-on-one meetings, including one with all his direct reports. Except for the meeting with Scott and his meeting with Don Kelley at the Livonia plant, McGrath met each person in his own office and made it clear that he was in charge.

For the second week, he called for an 8 a.m. Monday morning meeting of all his direct reports and requested representation from the other departments as well. McGrath published no topic or agenda, but strongly suggested everyone should attend. While he had only asked the sales department to send a representative, Bud, Ray and Michael all showed up, curious to see him in action. The conference room table sat 12 and overflowed with every company manager present except John Anderson.

McGrath began, "Well men, (then noticing Denise, Kathy and Marie) and ladies, I hope we're going to work together for a long time and I thought we ought to get to know each other. We're growing quickly and transitioning from being a small company to a big company. We have to develop more formal ways of communicating, so I'd like to have this meeting every day."

There had always been a morning production meeting. Jimmy met with Terry, Karl, Denise and the daytime production supervisors to talk about the day's issues. It was a quick stand-up meeting held in front of the manufacturing bulletin board. They were amicable affairs that discussed and resolved potential problems. Sometimes a front office manager would attend if something affected them.

"I've formed some pretty good impressions about you, but you're probably curious about me. Well, I spent four years in the Army and left with the rank of Captain. Now I have worked in manufacturing companies for 25 years. I want you to remember one thing. In this company, excellent performance is standard, standard performance is substandard and I don't allow sub-standard performance to exist. Here is the agenda that I'd like to follow every day."

McGrath split a short stack of paper into two halves and passed each part down one side of the table. "Take a look at the outline and then let's work our way down the list of topics."

As each manager reviewed the one-page outline, McGrath picked up a white pencil eraser lying on the table in front of him and began to roll it around in his hands. "OK," he said, "let's talk about what we're making today."

"There really isn't anything to talk about there," Mack said. "The computer Material Requirements Planning System tells us what we need to make and we post the Master Production Schedule on the bulletin board outside of the Quality office. That's how everybody knows what we're supposed to produce."

"Then how do **I** know what we're producing?" McGrath said, aggressively, emphasizing the word "I".

"You can look it up on the computer anytime you want," Scott volunteered. "That should have been one of the reports that Kathy showed you yesterday." Kathy nodded that it was.

The tone of Scott's voice sounded innocent and helpful enough, but in reality, it was a jab at McGrath's lack of computer literacy. Until this meeting, only Scott and Kathy knew this fact. Michael quickly made the link between Scott's remark and the frustrated look he saw on Kathy's face as she returned to her office after McGrath's computer orientation.

Scott was amazed at how easily McGrath brushed off the suggestion that he could run his own report. Finally, Denise suggested that she could put a copy in his mail slot every morning after she posted a copy on the bulletin board. "Bingo," McGrath said, and that became the new procedure.

Some people say the true agenda of every meeting is a secret and an hour later, Scott left the meeting concluding the hour was for no other purpose than for McGrath to assert he was in charge.

A few hours later, Ken, Scott, Terry and Karl sat in a bar near the plant having lunch.

Karl asked, "Vot did you think of our new COO's meeting this morning?"

Scott opened, "I counted that he said "Bingo" twelve times."

Ken added, "He sure sent a strong message that he's in charge."

"The sub-standard performance part made me a bit uneasy," Terry added.

"He said the same thing in his talk vith the hourly verkers," Karl said.

Scott turned to Terry, "I was uncomfortable with it too. What bothers you about it?"

"I think it could cause people to hide defects. Sub-standard isn't allowed to exist? If you want to keep your boss happy, are you going to report a problem? When something is wrong, we want people to raise a red flag. We want to find the root cause of errors. We don't want people to hide stuff."

"Vot you say makes sense," Karl said. "I hope this guy didn't just do us more harm than good."

Fairlane Tool and Manufacturing. Co.
Organizational Chart
As of February 1990

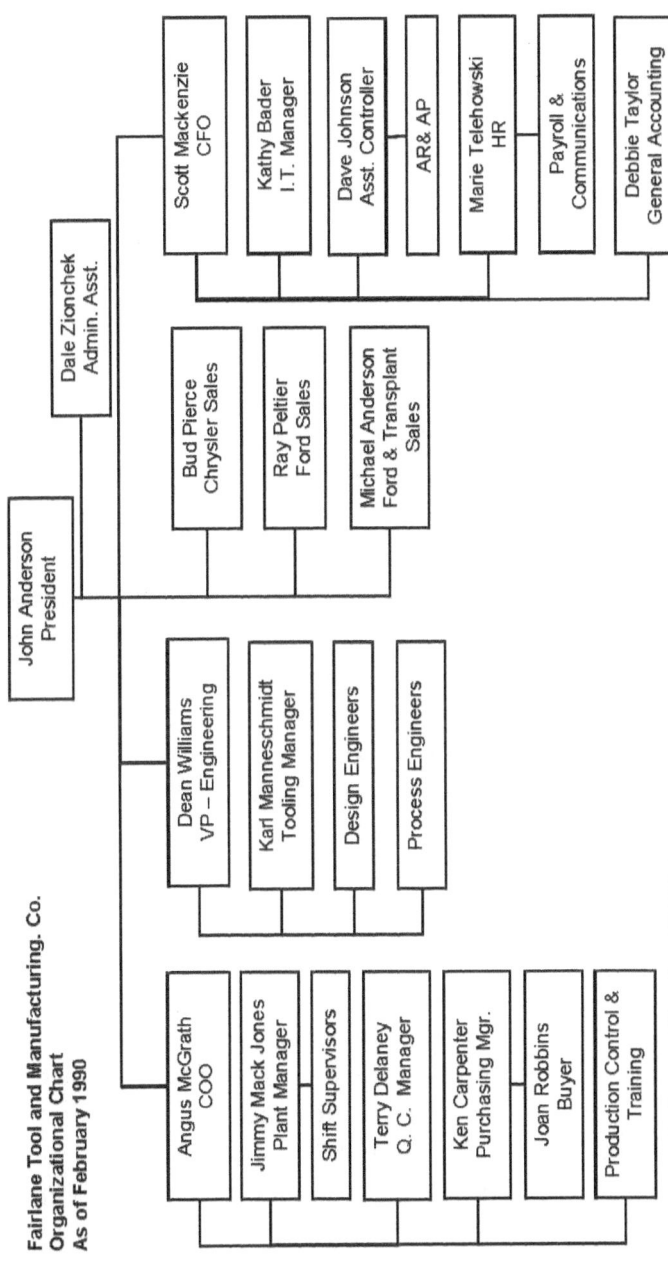

C://Administration/Personnel/Org-Chart-022890.doc

Chapter 22

The Lunch Buddy

Wednesday, February 28, 1990

After the waitress delivered cocktails and two trays of hors d'oeuvres, Scott closed the door and everyone took their places for the quarterly management meeting. While the seating varied some at every meeting, the positioning was mostly predictable. John Anderson always sat at the head of the table. Terry, the only smoker, sat at the opposite end. Having been the first to arrive, he went to the hotel bar beforehand for a bourbon, or perhaps two, and his face bore a decidedly mellow look. To avoid getting the smoke too near Bud, two seats away, who detested cigarettes, Terry pushed his chair three or four feet back from the table. Periodically taking a puff, Terry exhaled towards the room's back corner while tapping the ashes into an ashtray he held on his lap.

Even when he chaired a meeting, Scott habitually sat in the middle of the table facing the door.

McGrath sat on Anderson's right with the table's lone empty seat on McGrath's other side. John opened the meeting.

"It is good to have everyone here again. I'm glad we have everyone present. A few years ago, we only had five people at this meeting, yet today we have eleven for the first time. A year from now, twelve seats might not be enough."

John paused for dramatic effect, inspiring Terry to lift his glass in a toast. "To growth!"

John picked up his merlot and repeated "To growth!" as did other managers sitting at the table. "They say it's lonely at the top," he continued. "I started this company with just a few of the contracts from Silent Tool and a lot of time I felt I was alone in making this business a success. Many times, I have wished I had someone at my own level to talk to. I was lucky enough a few weeks ago to meet Bull McGrath, someone who has experience running a big company division. While I don't expect our company will ever be as big an operation as Bull has run, I have aspirations that we will be a lot bigger someday and I'm glad that he has consented to give us the benefit of his experience. So, anyhow, I'm glad I finally have someone at my own level to have lunch with!"

Again, John paused for dramatic effect. He looked at McGrath with real admiration and McGrath smiled with satisfaction at the words John said about him. This time neither Terry nor anyone else proposed a toast. In fact, this speech offended nearly everyone at the table. The reaction was stunned silence.

Anderson particularly offended Terry and Karl who came from Silent Tool with him to start the company when he said, "I felt that I was alone in making this business a success." Anderson offended Scott by the inference that John considered Bull more skilled than the other managers. Michael couldn't believe his brother had made such a gaffe and in reality, the only person who wasn't offended was Ray who really did consider himself inferior to McGrath.

Even though John did not offend Ray, Ray looked at Scott for his reaction. Scott looked across the table to Dean who was looking at Karl whose eyes were locked high on the wall above the sideboard. Each reacted with the stony silence required of an employee whose boss has deeply insulted him. Everyone clearly understood the implication of having McGrath as John's lunch buddy and that it made John genuinely happy. To more than one person, realizing John considered McGrath his equal brought Anderson down several levels in their estimation.

Since no one else had proposed a toast to McGrath, Anderson himself raised his glass to welcome him to the company. Without raising his elbow from the table, Terry raised his glass but did not drink. Scott raised his glass to his lips but did not sip whereas Michael finished off the rest of his gin and tonic and pushed the glass to the middle of the table thinking, *It's going to be a long night.*

"You are probably wondering about the new organizational structure," Anderson said. Opening up a manila folder, he pulled out copies of an organizational chart and passed them around. John had always discussed past organizational changes with Scott, Dean and Jimmy, but the new organizational chart surprised Scott. First, John had not consulted him and second, human resources maintained the organizational chart and Marie had given him no indication that John was working on any changes. Looking at the page passed to him, Scott realized Dale must have created this organizational chart because she formatted it differently and it contained the full file path name in the lower left-hand corner, a telltale sign of Dale's work.

The new org chart was significantly different. It showed McGrath, Dean and Scott reporting to John Anderson, but now Don, Ken and Denise reported to McGrath, not Jimmy, and it showed Terry reporting to McGrath instead of Dean. Scott looked around the table trying to determine how many of the affected people seemed to have had previous knowledge of these changes. By the end of the evening, he would conclude that McGrath and Dean were the only people John consulted about the moves ahead of time.

The level of enthusiasm was definitely lower than usual for the rest of the evening. Jimmy, in particular, who was normally a prodigious eater, seemed to have little appetite. He ate only half of his prime rib and uncharacteristically refused dessert.

Leaving the hotel that night, Terry's eyes met Karl's and Karl shook his head. The two talked privately in the parking lot as they stood by Terry's pick-up truck.

Scott had time to think on his way home. Pulling into his cold garage, he rifled through their green plastic recycling bin until he found the Tuesday Wall Street Journal and the Sunday Detroit News want ads and pulled them from the pile. Tucking them under his arm, he went into the living room and informed Mary that he was thinking he had spent enough time with this particular company.

Chapter 23

The Clothes Horse

Friday, March 16 1990

There was no question about it. Michael Anderson was a clothes horse. At 6'1" with blonde hair, blue eyes, a slim waist and a handsome face, Michael looked good in everything he wore and was fastidious about his appearance. Every day he wore a freshly pressed shirt and even when he bought a new shirt, he always had the cleaners wash and press it to get rid of the fold marks before he wore it.

Michael paid attention to fashion trends, but never followed fashion fads. When colored shirts with white colors became fashionable, he wore them, but his tastefully conservative attire always looked expensive even though he did not necessarily pay a lot for what he wore. Michael enjoyed shopping for clothes and had an eye for a bargain. He owned a distinctive camel overcoat that was obviously very expensive, even though he had purchased it for half price at an end of the season sale.

Within the company, only John and Scott came anywhere near the quality of Michael's wardrobe. John cared about what he wore only because he understood the impression clothes made on other people. He didn't like shopping for clothes and thus Barbara chose everything for him. Even when he bought a suit, she took him to the store and made selections for him as John fidgeted through the process. John's only input occurred when Barbara tried to buy him colored shirts with white collars. He steadfastly refused to look at them, insisting on shirts made from a single fabric. Tall and solid himself, John was consistently "tastefully conservative".

Scott wears nice suits to work every day only because John Malloy's best-selling business book **Dress for Success** said wearing suits improves effectiveness. Ever practical in nearly all matters, Scott viewed suits as a uniform he wore to work. If a shirt looked clean, but was a little rumpled, he saw no reason why he shouldn't wear it a second or third day. In any given year, he might buy two or three suits, always good quality garments on sale, but then he would keep them until they eventually wore out, usually due to wearing a hole in the crotch. This aggravated him because it seemed like a waste to retire a perfectly good suit jacket because the pants were no longer wearable. He found a tailor at one store who came up with the idea of adding extra lining material to the crotch, extending the suit's life. When he found a store that would sell him two pairs of pants with each jacket, he was finally able to balance the whole suit's useful life.

In many places people say "if you don't like the weather, wait an hour and it will change." The phrase is common in Michigan, too, but it is not necessarily an accurate statement. Michigan skies can be overcast for days with little apparent change. However, sometimes all four seasons happen in 24-hours.

This was one of those days. It was a cold winter morning when Michael left for work, but a cloudless day soon made everything seem like spring was on its way. The afternoon was so warm and gorgeous that Michael casually grabbed his coat and slung it over his arm as he headed home.

The next day, waking to another cold morning, Michael put on the camel coat again to find it was an extraordinarily poor fit. Not understanding what was wrong at first, he tested the sleeve length and the girth. This coat was obviously for a much larger, bulkier man. He put his hands in the pockets and found a set of keys. He examined the unfamiliar keys. *Ok, this is somebody else's overcoat.* His mind ran through the possibilities. He had never seen anyone else with a coat like this at Fairlane. If it wasn't his, whose was it? *MCGRATH! If I've got his keys, how did he get home? McGrath's company car hadn't arrived yet so there wouldn't be a second set of keys hanging in the office. If he drove his personal car, how would he get home?*

Michael sheepishly walked into McGrath's office a half hour later, apologizing profusely. McGrath explained that his wife drove the 25 miles each way to pick him up the night before. Since it had not occurred to him to tell her to bring the second set of keys to his car when she came to pick him up, she then had to drive him 25 miles each way to Fairlane the next morning. While McGrath seemed gracious on the surface, Michael thought he appeared to be doing a bad job at hiding that he was really pissed off. Michael knew he started off on the wrong foot with the new COO.

Chapter 24

Productivity is Down

Monday, April 9 1990

Denise's knees complained as she eased herself down the steel stairs leading from the production office, carrying the week's Master Production Schedule, a calculator, note pad and pen for McGrath's morning meeting. She had yet to figure out why they had the daily meeting. *Jimmy and I did just fine with production planning before he came. That man doesn't do anything but waste my time.*

Thirty seconds after Denise passed his door, Terry Delaney exited the Quality Control office, thinking remarkably similar thoughts. At least the meeting now involved only McGrath's direct reports. The other departments now only joined a weekly meeting on Tuesdays.

An hour after his counseling session with Barbara, John settled in behind the desk of his second-floor office. Having seen him pass through accounting, Scott entered John's office a few minutes later with the March financial statements.

"Whoa! What happened to our bottom line?" The numbers clearly surprised John. "This is half of where we should have been for last month."

Scott sat next to him at John's round table. "Two key things: McGrath's salary and benefits cost us $16,500 a month and we had a productivity drop. We had been running at a hundred-two to a hundred-five percent of standard. Now, all of a sudden, we dropped to ninety-seven percent."

"What jobs had the productivity drop?"

"Nothing stands out. A lot of different jobs dropped a little. We keep track of job set-up and run time separately and they're both down. Also, non-productive time is way up."

"I'll have Bull look into it."

"I'm wondering if he's the cause."

"Why do you say that?"

"What else has changed?"

"I don't know, but I bet Bull can figure it out."

In the weekly meeting the next day, McGrath was all over the productivity issue and laid the blame squarely on Jimmy's shoulders. Jimmy was speechless. *How does this guy expect me to run a plant when Denise and I are wasting an hour every day in this meeting?*

Most manufacturing personnel rarely went into the offices and most of the office people rarely went into the plant. Anybody hired in the last year, knew Marie Telehowski because she began their orientation. Ken Carpenter was in the plant a lot due to the nature of his purchasing job. Since Ken worked his way up from the plant floor, Ken was almost one of them.

Scott was in the plant a lot, often practicing "management by walking around." If he knew you, sometimes he'd stop and ask you how you were. He'd wave as he passed your workstation. Sometimes Scott would have a problem he was trying to figure out and would seek someone out to ask a question. He would explain the thing he was trying to understand so you didn't wonder why he wanted the information. He didn't know everybody, but he knew everybody who had been around for a few years.

Most of the hourly workers had not personally met Bull McGrath, but they disliked him anyhow. Anybody could tell. When an executive has a good relationship with hourly workers, they make eye contact with you when they walk through a plant or, perhaps, they'll wave. Nobody did that with Bull McGrath. They had already figured out that you were better off if he didn't know who you were.

Chapter 25

Financing

Wednesday, June 20, 1990

Ten weeks passed since John hired McGrath and Fairlane's problems got deeper and more varied. While McGrath managed to get productivity back to 100%, customer rejects increased and profitability continued to be below projections, even after revising the budget for McGrath's salary and benefits. The source of each month's budget overrun moved around but was always in some operations area. The budget overruns caused constant friction between McGrath and Mackenzie. Every month, Scott focused on that month's problem and every month McGrath blamed everyone but himself.

Since joining Fairlane, Scott had quarterly meetings with Comerica Bank. John attended any bank meeting of any significance and for the last five quarters, every bank meeting was significant. Scott did the play by play and John did the color commentary, two voices telling a unified story.

Neither may have noticed, but one thing had changed. Scott's agenda for the March bank assigned John to explain McGrath's hiring and the profitability decline. John fumbled the explanation and Scott made no effort to support John's decision. Their two voices were now telling two slightly different stories.

It can take years for a company to build a banking relationship. Getting a business loan is far more complicated than just giving a bank financial statements and projections. The bank would like evidence that the management team is competent, and the projections will come true. They must understand the company's story.

Jack Porter had been the bank's loan officer for almost eight years, an unusually long tenure for a middle-market loan officer to be responsible for an account. Bankers normally move either up or out. Knowing this, Scott consciously managed the risk that someone else could take over Fairlane's account at any time. He tried to have Porter bring at least one other bank person with him to every meeting, particularly since he knew that it was other people behind the scenes, not Porter, who made the decisions about Fairlane's loans.

No one person has complete decision-making authority over bank loans. Different people play different roles. At most banks, loan officers like Porter are primarily salespeople. It is their job to bring their bank lending opportunities. Bank customers deposit money in a bank, sometimes receiving interest, sometimes not and the banks then lend that money to businesses and individuals at a higher interest rate, paying their expenses and making a profit from the spread, or difference, in the interest rates. Banks lend dollars to make pennies.

Leverage is a measure of risk. Compared to their borrowers, banks are highly leveraged. Leverage is determined by an organization's balance sheet[4]. A balance sheet shows what an organization owns (their assets), what they owe (their liabilities) and the difference between the two (their equity). A bank would generally want a manufacturing company like Fairlane to have a ratio of

---

[4] An individual's balance sheet is called a *Statement of Net Worth*.

liabilities to equity, usually called a debt/equity ratio, of no more than two to one.

Because banks invest other people's money, they are highly regulated and regulators do not allow them to lend money in high-risk situations. The whole bank lending process is structured around making sure the bank has a relatively secure position every time it makes a loan.

No one person can make a bank lending decision. Every bank loan officer has a counterpart called a credit officer who performs a quality control function on business lending. At some banks, if the loan officer and the credit officer agree, they make a loan with their joint authority. At other banks, the loan officer's boss (often called a loan group head) and the credit officer's boss (called a credit group head) must also sign off. At Comerica, Porter served in an advisory role. He could make recommendations, but the other three people really made the lending decision.

Because Scott understood this, he tried to have Porter bring at least one other person to every quarterly meeting. This time, Porter was due to bring the loan group and credit group heads, two of the three decision-makers on Fairlane's bank relationship.

When the bank brought three people, Fairlane would bring three people. John and Scott agreed this strategy demonstrated the depth of Fairlane's management team. Dean, Mack, Don and Dave had all attended bank meetings at least once. Since three people would represent the bank, John suggested they also bring Bull McGrath. *This ought to be interesting,* Scott thought. He figured, as long as McGrath got the same coaching he gave John before every bank meeting, they would be okay.

John, Scott and McGrath sat around John's round table to plan for the bank meeting. Scott opened the discussion,

"Today, we're going to have the loan group head, Bruce Davis, the credit group head, Dan Wollschlager, and as always, our loan officer, Jack Porter. It's been nine months since either Bruce or Dan have visited, so our main purpose will be to talk about our three-year revenue projections and the lending we'll need to support additional equipment, receivables and inventory."

Early in the discussion, it became apparent that McGrath had never been in a bank meeting. It made sense. Because he had always worked in operations management for big companies, the CFO, Treasurer and others had always handled banking. Since this meeting was well out of McGrath's comfort zone, he was willing to listen, learn and take his assigned task of giving the plant tour and talking about equipment needs.

Since Fairlane had now missed its projections for three months in a row, it could have been a tough meeting. But, in a manufacturing plant, McGrath projected an air of competence and authority even managing to come off as a likeable character. "Thank God," Scott thought. "We've managed to keep the bank happy for another quarter."

Chapter 26

New Ark

Thursday, June 21, 1990

Everyone working for McGrath had learned that he didn't want anyone to be a problem bringer and that any bad news messenger was likely to be out the door within a month. No one wanted to be the person who brought up a problem in a meeting. Thus, everyone learned to bring McGrath good news and bury bad news anywhere they could.

The people most likely to see operational problems all worked for McGrath. Terry Delaney's quality control staff had become more likely to let marginal quality pass inspection. Jimmy's manufacturing personnel became increasingly likely to see problems and say, "It's not my job" and Denise Bridges no longer had time to follow the company's inventory cycle counting procedure.

The few people who didn't work for McGrath worked for Scott, Dean or John. Due to the nature of what accounting does, Scott became increasingly vocal about manufacturing's declining profitability and the contempt he and McGrath had for each other increased by the month.

The hinges Fairlane shipped to Chrysler's Newark, Delaware assembly plant stood out as the company's most persistent quality problem. Dean and Karl studied the problem personally and both concluded the root cause was faulty tooling set-up in Fairlane's Dearborn plant coupled with a failure to catch the problem in-house due to the consequences of McGrath punishing anyone who brought him bad news. Quality manager Terry Delaney knew that some press operators were ignoring the company's statistical quality control procedures, but Terry's pleas proved to be far less convincing than McGrath's subtle threats. Terry surreptitiously discussed the issue with Dean, his former boss. Dean received assurances, but no action, from McGrath.

Delaney's repeated promises to correct the problem left him with no credibility with Chrysler plant personnel. Therefore, the next customer call went to John Anderson who transferred it to McGrath. The situation called for a high-level customer plant visit. As a result, McGrath chewed out Delaney, and told him he would go to the plant himself and fix the problem for good.

McGrath began by calling the plant manager at Newark assembly. Since the plant generated significantly more revenue in a week than Fairlane produced in a year there was no reason why the Chrysler executive should have talked to McGrath, but miraculously he smooth-talked himself into a telephone conversation. In a short time, McGrath arranged not only meetings with the plant's key quality personnel for the next afternoon but also golf and dinner with the plant manager afterwards.

Delaney gave McGrath advice on getting to the Delaware plant, telling him to fly into Philadelphia and take a cab. He also briefed him about pronouncing the city's name. "Newark, New Jersey is pronounced *New-work*, Newark, Ohio is pronounced *Nerk*, but, Newark, Delaware is pronounced *New Ark*," Delaney said.

Debbie grumbled at the cost of McGrath's first class, short notice tickets to Philadelphia on US Airways.

The following morning, McGrath pulled his new company vehicle, an Eddie Bauer limited edition Ford Explorer, up to the curb in front of the Smith Terminal at Detroit Metro Airport. A curb-check baggage handler took his golf clubs and garment bag and gave him two luggage claim tickets. McGrath gave him a five-dollar tip and entered the terminal. He compared the time on his watch with the departure time on his ticket and decided to kill some of the time by getting a haircut at the barbershop near the ticket area. With one empty chair, the idle barber seated him immediately. With time remaining he went through security, bought a black coffee and a Detroit Free Press, finishing the coffee and arriving at his gate only minutes before the boarding call for first-class passengers.

The plane was barely in the air when a sinking realization hit him. He didn't remember parking the Explorer! He took the bags out of his trunk, gave them to the baggage handler, walked into the terminal, got a haircut but he didn't remember parking his car. He must have left it sitting at the curb!

He could feel his blood pressure rise. His face flushed and he gritted his teeth, mad at himself and mad at the situation. This indeed was a major screw-up. They would certainly tow his car. He would need to get somebody at the office to track it down and get it out of the impoundment lot.

Landing what seemed like an eternity later, McGrath went to the nearest pay phone to call someone at Fairlane. Ken Carpenter seemed like the person most likely to be discreet about the blunder. Ken could barely contain his laughter as he heard the story over the phone but managed a serious tone until he hung up with McGrath.

Calling airport security, Ken was able to talk to a real person with surprising speed and shared a good laugh with security about the bonehead move his boss had made. Quickly, Ken identified the Explorer's location and learned that it would cost $100 to get the car back.

In the meantime, McGrath waited at baggage claim for his garment bag and golf clubs. He knew this was going to be an exceptionally bad day when the belt stopped without producing his luggage. Returning to the pay phone, he called again and learned Ken would retrieve the SUV within the hour.

Stifling his laughter, Ken went into Scott's office and arranged to borrow his company car. Scott then gave Debbie a hand-written note authorizing the impound lot expenditure, noting its "confidential" nature. She managed to remain composed as she gave Ken $100 out of petty cash for the fee but broke out laughing as she got in Scott's car to drive Ken to the impound lot.

Angry with more than just his missing luggage, McGrath practically threw his claim tickets across the counter in the US Airways office. The woman behind the counter handled him professionally and looked at his luggage claim tickets. There was a long pause as she stared at the small paper slips stapled to his ticket envelope.

"This says you checked your bags through to Philadelphia," she said.

A bit bewildered, McGrath looked around the office for some kind of sign and asked, "Well, where am I?"

"Pittsburgh," she responded. "You must have another leg to your trip."

The claim agent determined McGrath had now missed his connecting flight by ten minutes. The next flight would leave in two hours, making him at least a half hour late for his initial meeting. He resolved to tell the customer there was a flight delay and not to tell anyone at the company about this second screw up lest they consider him a complete idiot.

Debbie returned with the Sable just in time for Scott and Dave to take it for their quarter planning meeting at the Fairlane Club sports bar. As CPAs, they both needed 40 hours of continuing professional education (CPE) each year and discussing what courses Dave should take was frequently part of the agenda. Both Scott and Dave prepared for the meeting by marking up Michigan Association of CPAs course catalogs.

When the planning portion of lunch was over, Dave took a sip of his beer and asked, "So what are you taking this year?"

"Mostly computer classes. Since IT reports to me, I figure I should keep up with what's going on in technology. It's been 7 years since I wrote a line of code and I feel rusty."

The classes that Scott planned to take sounded way over Dave's head. He knew Scott had worked in information systems for five years, but it surprised him that Scott even tried to keep up with a fast-changing field in which he no longer worked. The rest of the meal, they talked baseball.

Chapter 27

Restless Sleep

Wednesday, July 4, 1990

Every time a restless sleep took him back, Bull's brain replayed the same dream. As his wife slept beside him, he donned his helmet and flak-jacket. He draped a second one over his left arm to sit on, protecting his ass from gunfire through the chopper's unarmored floor. Buck ran a helicopter maintenance company, but when a pilot friend was short a door gunner, he jumped at the chance to go along for the ride.

Flying low, a VC patrol below fired at them and the other door gunner opened fire. Turning towards the threat, the pilot fired his side mounted 7.62 Gatling guns and Charlie fired back, bullets tearing through the metal all around them. With a dead co-pilot and a punctured engine block, they fell out of control and Buck awakened.

Outside the open bedroom window, a hard summer rain seemed peaceful compared to the violence of his dream. Buck stumbled to the bathroom in the darkness, orienting himself by placing his hand on the wall behind the toilet. He lifted the seat and broke wind before hearing the sound of water on water, confirming his aim.

The horror of the morning 22 years before did not end as quickly as the dream. The plunging chopper pitched him out the door at 35 feet. Falling through layers of foliage, he landed in thick black muck with three broken ribs, a broken left forearm and a multitude of bruises, abrasions and small puncture wounds.

He stifled the sound of his pain as his jubilant foe ran along the high ground above him toward the wrecked chopper seventy yards away. He could hear the paralyzed pilot's screams as the victors burned the chopper with him in it.

Sixteen days and 30 pounds later, he stumbled back to the safety of the forward most American base, seven days after his memorial service in West Virginia. As he drank clean water for the first time since the crash, his mother handed the Salvation Army the last of his personal mementos to avoid the daily reminder of her painful loss.

Bull put on his bathrobe and slippers. He plodded through the dark house and opened the door to the garage. He felt his way in the dark around Janelle's Dodge Caravan to the passenger side of his Explorer. The dome light seemed bright to his unadjusted eyes as he opened the vehicle door. He found a pack of filtered cigarettes on top of the owner's manual, removed one and returned the pack to the glove box. He took a match pack from a kitchen drawer as he passed through to the screened porch.

He rarely smoked. Only when he returned to 1968, did he feel the need. While the cigarette lasted, he sat watching and listening to the falling rain, wondering if the weather would wash out the family outing the next day. That was enough and he returned to bed.

On weekdays, Bull's clock radio always played WJR at 6 am. Unlike most holidays, he set the radio for a 7 am rise.

Mist rose as the sun warmed his wet asphalt driveway. As Buck walked to the *Detroit Free Press* tube at the street, he saw flags displayed on several neighbor's homes for the Independence Day holiday. Putting the paper on the kitchen table, he found their flag in the closet and inserted it into the bracket on the porch.

He did not need to coax his daughters to get ready for Cedar Pointe. At 8:10 am, their two girlfriends buckled themselves into the back of Janelle's minivan to depart for the amusement park. The girls chattered and laughed the entire two-hour drive. Buck and Janelle secretly listened. They learned more about their daughter's activities from the backseat conversation than from six months at the dinner table.

The chatter continued as they parked and Buck clicked "lock" on the van's key fob. He and Janelle walked in front of the girls toward the front gate. Other loud teenagers made the parking lot a noisy, high-energy environment.

Pop, pop, pop, pop, pop! Janelle looked to her right. Some boys had ignited a string of firecrackers. She turned to look at Buck and he was gone.

Dad! His mortified eldest daughter cried. Buck was on the ground in a ditch. Janelle helped her husband to his feet. Water, grass and mud spots covered his khaki slacks and white golf shirt. The sound was enough to take him back to the Army again.

Chapter 28
Contingency Planning

Thursday, August 2, 1990

"That's funny!" Debbie looked at a grainy black and white photo posted on the break room bulletin board. Ken walked over from the coffee maker to see what she was looking at. The picture showed a man in uniform giving Adolph Hitler a straight-armed salute. In pen, someone had written "Angus McGrath" and drawn an arrow to the man in uniform.

"It is funny," Ken said, looking over her shoulder.

"How did they make a picture of McGrath with Hitler," Debbie asked.

"That's not McGrath," Ken said. "It's Hermann Goering!"

The picture managed to stay on the bulletin board for a whole day before John discovered and removed it. In the meantime, almost everyone in the office saw it and understood that the company's COO not only acted like a Nazi dictator, he also resembled Hitler's right-hand man.

That evening, as Scott merged onto the Southfield freeway heading home, he pushed the fourth preset radio button in his Sable getting WWJ 950 AM radio, Detroit's all-news radio station. On July 17th, the Dow Jones Industrial Average had flirted with a 3000-point close before retreating 100 points. Scott hoped for some good news.

Somehow, the day's major news had not filtered into Fairlane's offices. Iraq had invaded Kuwait and the possibility of war was the only thing on the radio.

Sitting in the Dearborn Big Boy, Scott sipped Coke from a red plastic glass, posing a question to Dean, Michael and Ray. "Cars were selling at a 15 million rate at the beginning of the year and we started the summer at 14 million. What is Saddam's little adventure into Kuwait likely to do to us?"

"It can't be good," Dean responded. "Bush says there's no place for such naked aggression. We're sending planes, ships and troops there already. It looks like war to me."

"I agree with you," Michael said. "Saddam has a million battle-hardened veterans from his war with Iran. I can't imagine that he's going to back down when he has the home field advantage."

Terry asked, "When do you suppose this will happen?"

Dean responded, "The U.S. government learned its lesson in Vietnam. They're going to need six months to build up troops and supplies."

Michael added, "The U.S. military always attacks at midnight and they own the night. If we had moon charts for Baghdad, I bet we could figure this out to the day or maybe even the hour."

Scott said, "So I think I hear you guys saying that by February 2nd, we're going to be at war. What's that going to do to car sales?"

Terry interjected, "It's not going to be good. We might lose 15 percent if people were just generally nervous, 30% if they're worried and 50% if there is an outright panic."

"That's what I was thinking," Scott said. "I guess I'd better start running some contingency plans."

After lunch, Scott stopped in John's office. "Some of us were talking during lunch about this Iraq crisis and our consensus is that it could tank auto sales by 15-30 percent sometime soon. I think we ought to run some contingency plans."

McGrath walked in as Scott was talking. "I heard you say contingency plans. Are you thinking that the Middle East thing could hurt us?"

"I do, maybe by as much as 30%."

"I agree," McGrath responded.

"Well," John said, looking at McGrath, "what would you do about it?"

McGrath continued, "I've been through this before, first we freeze hiring and if we lose people, cover those positions as best we can until we know we've got this threat behind us and put contingency plans together in case it does happen."

"That all makes sense," Scott agreed. "I can get projections done by Friday."

As Mackenzie and McGrath left his office, John thought, *I'm glad they agree on something!*

Chapter 29

The First to Go

Monday, August 20, 1990

"I think we should call it "Bullshit Bingo," Michael said, showing Scott the list of words.

"Perhaps in an effort to mask a lack of actual knowledge, you can depend on McGrath to spew ten or fifteen of these terms in any given weekly meeting. To liven things up we need some kind of spreadsheet that will randomize these words on a Bingo sheet. Every time he says one of these words, you mark off a square. The first person to get five squares in a row wins."

"You can't just stand up and say 'Bingo' in the middle of a meeting. How do you let other players know you've won?"

"I haven't figured that out yet, but I figured you'd know how to create a spreadsheet that will randomize the game sheet."

"OK, I'll see what I can do. Instead of "Free" in the middle, I suppose we could use the word 'bingo' since he says it so often."

Scott got back to Michael in a few hours.

"I had trouble figuring out how to randomize a word list without the possibility of picking the same word twice. So, I added enough words to make an even hundred and put them in a ten by ten matrix. Based on the time you open Excel, the program chooses a starting point on five different rows giving you the Bingo Sheet. Also, since he says 'bingo' so many times himself, I don't think he would think it abnormal if the winner just worked the word into the conversation."

Michael had only been gone a moment when Jimmy stood in Scott's open door.

"Hey Scott, can I talk to you?"

"Of course. Have a seat."

"I just gave McGrath my two-weeks-notice, and I need to know what I need to know."

"What?"

"I quit, Scott. Life's too short to work for an asshole."

"Where are you going? Do you have a job?"

"Yeah, I'm going to RTW in Livonia.   Bigger responsibilities and more money."

In the next half hour, Scott heard Jimmy's litany of frustrations with McGrath. He had apparently failed to give him a raise of any kind in his last performance review, citing the decreased manufacturing productivity.   Jimmy suspected McGrath was a closet racist since his boss frequently talked down to him.

"Hard to do for someone who is six-foot-five," Scott said.

Jimmy recognized Scott was making a bad joke and smiled anyhow.

Scott explained Jimmy's options for his 401(k) and the terms of his stock buy-back. Their meeting ended with Scott saying, "Don't leave without saying goodbye, big guy. I'm going to miss you."

Scott went upstairs to John's office as soon as Jimmy was out of sight. Losing Jimmy also meant they would have to buy-back his stock. With Fairlane's cash flow problems, they would need to find another $142,000, which they didn't have, within 90 days. McGrath was in John's office and Scott entered without knocking.

Scott directed his frustrations at McGrath. "We've got a serious problem. Since you arrived, our inventory has ballooned to 39 days. Since the expansion had already maxed out our line of credit, this extra inventory has our accounts payable at 45 days. Where do you expect us to get another $142,000 to buy out Mack?"

"I'm working on it."

"You said that when our inventory was 37 days."

"I said I'm working on it and I have already been talking with someone who worked with me at Kelsey-Hayes," McGrath said.

"When did this happen? Mack said you he just told you this morning."

"It is something I've been working on."

"You mean you've been working on driving him out of the company?"

"No, I could see it coming. He wasn't hacking it."

"You are the one who isn't hacking it. It is beyond me how you think you can run a manufacturing plant in 1990 when you don't even know how to log onto your computer. You can blame other people as much as you want, but these problems are your responsibility."

Scott's tirade obviously angered McGrath who stepped aggressively toward him which accentuated their eight-inch height difference. Scott countered by taking John's guest chair and standing on it so that he now towered over McGrath.

"Hit me, you ugly playground bully," Scott suggested. "You know you want to."

McGrath's face grew red as he glared at Scott.

Until Scott got on the chair, John had simply been a passive observer as the heated argument went on in front of him.   Now, he got up to prevent an improbable fight between his two Vice Presidents, pushing McGrath away from the chair. He said, "Let's talk about this later Scott. We'll find the money; we'll find the money."

McGrath backed away, still glaring and John motioned for Scott to get down off the chair. John said, "We'll talk later Scott." His young CFO dismounted the chair, walked out the door and down the stairs.

"You let him provoke you," John said. "It isn't good for two people to get mad at the same time. Scott wasn't going to back down."

"You didn't need to get between us, John. I can handle myself."

"I wouldn't be so sure. I saw a situation like this once at a bar after a sports banquet. A tight end got kicked in the balls by a tailback who had been dancing on a chair. Scott has heard that story before and may have planned to do the same thing to you. He still pumps iron; you never have. If you touched him, he would have defended himself and I suspect he would have hit you fast and hard. From my vantage, point, you were looking pretty vulnerable."

McGrath shook his head and stormed out of the room.

Scott went back into John's office a few hours later. "A week ago McGrath proposed that we wouldn't do any hiring until this thing in Kuwait resolves. You, McGrath and I all agreed to it, as did all the other managers in the company. I don't think we need both a COO and a plant manager right now. I think we should stick to that plan. McGrath should run the plant and we shouldn't hire anybody new until this war resolves itself.

John didn't have to think about Scott's proposal. "I think that's a reasonable thing to do."

Therefore, that became the plan; McGrath would run the plant and they would save the cost of a plant manager's salary.

Chapter 30

Another Casualty

Monday, September 17, 1990

The big Monday morning news was that Denise had given McGrath notice that she was leaving Fairlane to join Mack at RTW. The news spread quickly throughout the company and Marie gave her a big hug when she came into the offices to check her mail slot. Denise went into Marie's office to work out some of the details of her separation. Marie was surprised to learn that she was only giving a single week's notice.

"Good lord. It has been hard being in the same office as that man for the last four weeks. I couldn't stand to spend two more."

With the hiring freeze, Marie learned that Brian, who did the hourly worker training, would take over Denise's job. It made sense. With a hiring freeze, there wasn't anybody to train, and Brian had handled her tasks several times in the past when she was sick or on vacation.

John came into Scott's office and slid a check onto his desk. "Here's a check for McGrath's buy-in. It will more than cover buying out Jimmy's 200 shares." Scott picked up the check from Comerica Bank. For other minority shareholders, Comerica had loaned the money to purchase stock and taken the stock as collateral. John owned 15,000 shares and the rest of the management team owned 1,500 shares combined with Dean and Scott being the second and third largest shareholders at just 300 shares each. Scott quickly did the math in his head. The check for $355,000 instantly bought McGrath the second largest interest in Fairlane.

Sure, McGrath's buy-in was still only a 3% ownership share, but it gave him options that were 50% higher than the company's two other long-tenured vice presidents. Scott was not happy about this development, but John was out of his office before he could formulate anything to say.

Chapter 31

Reasonable Accommodation

Friday, October 12, 1990

"I thought you should see these." Marie slid into Scott's guest chair, putting two pieces of paper in front of him. The pages were, not one, but two reprimands for Leroy Johnson, dated a week apart. He read the first write-up. Apparently, Leroy had reported production on a part numbered T9-16880-AA instead of a similar part number ending in 808-AA.

"It's a natural mistake," Scott said. "880-AA is probably a part Leroy works on all the time. 808-AA isn't all that common. Anyone could make this mistake. Besides, the guy's dyslexic, those numbers probably look the same to him."

The other write-up was for a similar issue.

"I think McGrath's preparing to fire him," Marie said.

"That's what it looks like to me too. He's trying to get three strikes on the poor guy."

"This is a real landmine. This is exactly what Congress intended the new *Americans with Disabilities Act* to prevent. It says we are supposed to make reasonable accommodations for people with handicaps."

"It's more than that," Scott said. "It's just not right."

A few minutes later, Scott and Marie were in McGrath's office. Scott opened while Marie listened, "It looks like you're trying to get rid of Leroy Johnson."

"I am. I've got the third write-up right here."

"Can you tell me why you want to do this?"

"He's constantly messing up his production reports. That messes up our inventory and it can't be tolerated."

"That didn't seem to be a problem when Mack and Denise were running manufacturing."

Scott's remark caused McGrath's cheeks to flush and he stood up behind his desk, accentuating his full eight inch height difference over Scott. Scott was not going to stand on a chair a second time. Marie tried to defuse the situation. "Denise knew the schedule and probably caught any of Leroy's errors before she entered them. Under the new law, Brian will have to do that, too."

"The law?" The statement surprised McGrath.

"Yes," she said. *"The Americans with Disabilities Act,* passed in July, says that we have to make a reasonable accommodation for a person's disability. Having Brian confirm that what he scheduled Leroy to produce agrees with Leroy's production report would be an example of a reasonable accommodation." She handed the two reprimands back to McGrath. "You should probably destroy these or the Labor Department could use them as evidence in court that you didn't provide a reasonable accommodation."

McGrath took the two reprimands from Marie plus the third that was already in his hand; he slowly and deliberately tore the stack twice, and tossed them in his wastebasket.

"Thank-you," Marie said, as she and Scott headed out the door.

A minute later, back in her office, Scott was beaming. "You were amazing, absolutely amazing. Thank-you."

Chapter 32

Captain Queeg

Saturday, November 10, 1990

Scott instigated the party. When Michael got one of the major roles in the Players annual full-length play, many people at Fairlane wanted to see it. When he invited John & Barbara Anderson, John offered to sponsor dinner and tickets to the show, adding that he would pay it out of his own pocket in view of the slowing auto sales as the country prepared for war. Scott used his pull with the club's office manager to get three front row tables and made dinner reservations for 18 at Tom's Oyster Bar.

Following Scott's directions, Marie guided Jack into the right hand lane as I-375 spilled into downtown Detroit.

"I think it's on the corner," she said, followed by "there are a couple of parking spots!" pointing to not one, but two metered spots two lanes to their right.

The sign in front of the restaurant advised that valet parking was available, but they drove around the block for the cheaper street parking. Jack and Marie had few "dress up" clothes. Jack wore the black suit that he usually reserved for weddings and funerals while Marie wore a simple black dress she felt fortunate to find on sale at Hudson's during her lunch break earlier in the week.

Scott described the event as "black tie optional" and advised Marie that Jack didn't need to wear a tuxedo, but a jacket and tie were required and that wearing a bow tie would make him feel like he fit in better. With a black suit and bow tie, at least from a distance, Jack looked like Scott, Michael, and Mark Bader in tuxedos standing by the bar.

Kathy and Mary Mackenzie sat on the barstools next to them. Kathy pulled Marie into the conversation about Mary's dress, a burgundy brocade gown under a short matching jacket with a black velvet collar.

"Can you believe she made this herself? Isn't it stunning!"

John and Barbara Anderson soon arrived. Barbara wore a simple gray evening gown that was far less expensive than what she would have worn for her affluent Franklin neighbors. "So what is this play about?" John asked Michael.

"It's a courtroom drama based on the novel **The Caine Mutiny** by Herman Wouk. The book won a Pulitzer Prize. The play is **The Caine Mutiny Court Martial** and just covers part of the book. You may have seen the movie starring Humphrey Bogart who plays paranoid Captain Queeg. Fred McMurray and Van Johnson co-star. McMurray plays an aspiring novelist, who stirs up doubt about the captain's capabilities with the rest of the officers. When Queeg is indecisive in the middle of a typhoon, Van Johnson takes over control of the ship."

"Oh, yeah," John responded. "Isn't this the one where Bogart keeps playing with some metal balls through the whole movie?"

"It is," Michael answered, adding, "playing Queeg got Bogart an academy award nomination, but he lost to Marlon Brando in **On the Waterfront**."

"So who are you playing?"

"I'm playing Steve Maryk, the Van Johnson role. Maryk is the first officer who takes control from the captain during the typhoon."

"Good for you," John said. "It sounds like a great part!"

John and Scott led the standing ovation at the end of the play, followed quickly by the rest of the Fairlane party. Marie and Kathy helped Mary Mackenzie serve the dessert she made while Michael got out of costume and scrubbed the make-up off his face. Barbara gave her brother-in-law a big hug as he came out from back stage to join the rest of the party. "Hey sailor, you look good in a naval uniform."

John shook his younger brother's hand. "That was a wonderful job. I'm really proud of you."

"Thanks John, that means a lot."

Chapter 33

Queeg's Balls

Monday, November 12, 1990

"Metal balls? Are those Queeg's metal balls?" Scott asked Michael on Monday morning.

"Well, they're not actually Queeg's balls," Michael answered, "but they're just like them. Chuck Roberts has the balls that we used in the show, but when I bought ball bearings for the props, I got some extras."

"Why are you showing them to me?" Scott asked.

"Well, I'm forming a little betting pool and I thought that you'd like a piece of the action. You know how McGrath always picks up whatever is on the table and plays with it during his weekly meeting?"

"Yeah."

"I want to start a betting pool on how long it will take him to pick them up at tomorrow's meeting. Closest one wins."

Scott broke into a huge knowing grin at the thought of having some fun at McGrath's expense. "Where do I sign up?"

"Actually, I wanted your advice on how we should do it. Do you think we should pick specific times or is there some other way that might work?

Scott mused, "One of the issues would be whether it would be a game of skill or luck. If you picked times, the first ten minutes of the meeting would probably be snapped up right away and you wouldn't get much money in the pot. How about if we did it like a football pool and assigned one-minute blocks to the 60-minute meeting. The times would be drawn at random and the time on the clock in the conference room would determine the winner."

"What if he doesn't pick them up?" Michael asked.

"I can't imagine that he wouldn't," Scott responded. "After all, you remember that time that somebody left the really big rubber band on the table. He kept snapping it and plucking it all meeting. Just in case though, we could say that there would be carryover to the next meeting if he didn't pick them up tomorrow."

"I like this," said Michael.

"Me too," said Scott. "I'll take the first 10 squares when you've got it done."

Tuesday, November 13, 1990

All the salespeople agreed McGrath's weekly operations meeting was "a bullshit waste of time". Originally, McGrath wanted all three of them there, but since they worked for John, not McGrath, they had quickly managed to arrange for having a department representative rather than all three salespeople.

Whichever sales person was representing the company each week usually arrived at the weekly meeting at least ten minutes late, but the next day, not only were all three present but everyone was at least five minutes early. McGrath walked in at 7:58 and was startled to see all three sales people, particularly, a few minutes early.

"What got all you guys here so early?" McGrath asked. "Free doughnuts?"

Since there obviously weren't any doughnuts on the table, the question was a little awkward. Michael anticipated this and said, "Actually, there are some sales opportunities out there we thought this group should know about, so we'd like to give a brief update about what we're working on."

"OK," McGrath said, "but no more than ten minutes total." With that, he picked up the steel balls from the glass ashtray that Michael had placed 18 inches in front of his usual head of the table seat. The move was so quick that it startled everyone. Scott, who was sitting at the other end of the long rectangular table opposite McGrath, looked up at the clock. It was 7:59 AM. McGrath hadn't even sat down. The sixty-minute time block on the fully subscribed grid hadn't even started. McGrath looked around silently at the baffled faces of the attendees. Had someone told him? Did he know?

Scott searched McGrath's face for clues and then the faces of the other people in the room.

No, Scott concluded. *He suspects that something is up but has no idea what it is.* Then McGrath started grinding the balls, one over another in his left hand. It was just like in the play and there were five people in the room who had seen it and another three who were in the betting pool, yet now they would have to wait a full hour to talk about what happened.

In front of him were the previous month's efficiency reports. For the 9th month in a row, customer rejects were up and McGrath was not pleased. Rather than shouldering any responsibility for the performance, it was clear that he was looking for a scapegoat and he was looking directly at Tom Hickey, the second shift production supervisor who had come in outside his shift to attend the weekly meeting.

"Mr. Hickey, in this plant, excellent performance is standard, standard performance is sub-standard, and sub-standard performance is not permitted to exist."

Marie was mortified. Fairlane had its own Captain Queeg, rolling two steel ball bearings over and over again in his hands. She paid little attention that next hour, thinking mostly about how horrible it was to be in a company where 80% of the people worked for such a tyrant.

When the meeting ended at 9:10 a.m., McGrath put both balls in his suit pants pocket and strode out of the room to his office next door. Scott had to rush to another meeting, but Michael Anderson and the other sales personnel had a good time talking about what had happened in Michael's office upstairs. Michael was able to catch up with Scott for lunch.

"I can't believe he delivered Queeg's actual lines," Michael said.

"Too bad this isn't the Navy," Scott responded. "I'd love to have him just disappear over the side of the ship."

Chapter 34

Revised Projections

Wednesday, January 16, 1991

Scott and Dave sat side-by-side working on budget revisions. "How grim do they look?" Scott asked.

"Pretty grim. Weekly automotive sales have edged down every month since August. We've a major product launch postponed and a couple of assembly plants cut shifts. I'm thinking we're going to be down 30% until this Kuwait thing gets resolved."

"I agree. The UN deadline was yesterday, but so far, nothing seems to be happening, but it looks like something could happen any day now. In the meantime, it looks like McGrath laying off 30 people in November was absolutely the right move. I hated to do it so close to Christmas, but our cash is really tight."

"How have the calls with the steel companies been going?" Dave asked.

"Amazingly well. Yeah, they're nervous that we're paying them in 55 days, but they seem to understand what's going on."

Chapter 35

The Secret

Thursday, January 17, 1991

Scott and Kathy had a secret. Marie was sure of it. From her very first days at Fairlane, they always had what seemed to be an unusually close relationship for co-workers, but in the last few months, Marie noticed subtle changes in their behavior patterns. In Marie's first year with the company, Scott and Kathy's office doors were always open except when they left for the day. Now, one would often go into the other's office and close the door. Kathy's door had a glass panel, and Marie sometimes saw Scott sitting in her guest chair with the two of them having an animated conversation. Before, Kathy rarely went out to lunch, and when she did, it was always to run errands. Scott had always eaten with some subset of the same group of a dozen male management-level team members. Now it seemed like he and Kathy were eating out together at least once a week.

Sizing up the facts, it looked like they might be having an affair. Marie thought about the situation. Both Scott and Kathy were married. Mary Mackenzie was a very attractive woman and Mark Bader was a very handsome man. She had seen both couples together on several occasions and noticed no sign of marital stress. She had also observed Scott interacting with Mark and Kathy interacting with Mary. Scott and Mark had been roommates at Michigan. Marie never saw Scott flirt with Kathy. Still, something had changed, something secret, and Marie wondered what it was.

Independently, Dave had made similar observations. His audit training told him that an affair between an IT Manager and a CFO was a major audit risk. Without telling anyone else, he decided to check a few things out. Scott and Dave had a quarterly planning luncheon. Scott probably did the same with Kathy and Marie, but Scott and Kathy were eating together far more than that. If the lunches had a business purpose, the meals should show up on expense reports. Dave looked at Scott and Kathy's expense reports and saw nothing. Thus, the lunches were personal. If these weren't business lunches, why were the other people Scott normally ate lunch with never present?

Dave saw an opportunity one morning when he saw Kathy stick her head in Scott's office and ask if he had time for lunch that day. He also heard them agree to a 12:30 p.m. time. At 12:25, Dave put on his coat and told the receptionist he was going to run some errands, checking himself out until 1:30. Then he sat in the corner of the parking lot, pretending to look at his calendar while frequently glancing at his rear view mirror. A few minutes later he saw them get into Scott's Sable. Giving them a small head start, he followed, grateful that he drove a black Ford sedan, the most unlikely car to stand out in Dearborn. If they were going to a motel, they would have most likely turned right. Instead, they turned left towards downtown Dearborn.

When he saw Scott turn into a business, Dave turned into a gas station fifty yards behind them. They got out and went inside. Dave couldn't read the sign from this angle. He pulled out into traffic and continued driving down the street. It was a Middle Eastern restaurant specializing in vegetarian meals. While Scott didn't usually eat in this kind of place, the food choice was completely in keeping with

Kathy's dietary preferences. Nobody else on the management team would likely go to this place, which was probably part of the plan.

Dave and Marie never shared their observations with each other, but both kept watching for more clues to the mystery.

As Scott turned North on the Southfield Freeway at 5:35, he turned on WWJ for the traffic reports and once again found that the day's news had not filtered into Fairlane Tool. American planes were bombing targets in Iraq and a real shooting war had started. Suggesting that his daughters enjoy a computer math game, Scott and Mary turned on the living room television to watch the news.

The television showed grainy green hued videos of missiles destroying Baghdad buildings. Mary asked, "When would this have happened?"

"I don't know. I think it would be a seven to nine hour time difference, but I can probably figure it out." Returning from the multipurpose room that served as their combination office, children's play area and Mary's sewing room, he carried a World Almanac and a National Geographic World Atlas. Consulting both, he concluded, "It looks like seven hours. They said this started at 3 a.m. local time, so last night our time."

"It's a scary time."

Chapter 36

The Worst Day Ever

Monday, January 21, 1991

Scott was still in his overcoat as he walked into the lobby Monday morning. As he passed the glass receptionist window, Kim Newman was looking through it towards the parking lot with a sense of urgency on her face. She was on the phone with someone and beckoned to Scott to come right away. He arrived at her desk two seconds later as Kim was putting the call on hold.

"It's Mrs. Williams and she's really upset. She needs to talk to Dean right away and he's not here, yet. She asked to talk to you instead, line 2."

Kathy, whose office was across from the receptionist desk had heard some of the conversation and was now standing in her office door with an alarmed look on her face. Scott stepped into her office and Kathy closed the half glass door behind them as Scott picked up the receiver on her desk phone and hit line 2."

"Carol it's me, Scott. What's going on?"

Kathy couldn't hear Carol's end of the conversation but Scott's response told her it was awful.

"Oh God, no! Carol, I'm so sorry!" Tears started streaming down his face and he pulled several tissues from the box on Kathy's desk.

Just then, Dean walked in from the reception area with a concerned look on his face. Scott said softly into the phone. "Dean's here," and handed him the phone. He and Kathy left her office, closed the door and went into Marie's office next door. By now everyone in the office knew that something was going on but they hung back knowing that the situation was developing quickly and that they had better stay out of the way for the moment.

Kathy and Marie looked at him intently as Scott wiped his eyes and blew his nose, seemingly searching for words. "Somebody murdered Dean and Carol's daughter, Brenda, at Purdue last night. Carol didn't know much, but she was probably out jogging. We've got to get Dean home right away. He shouldn't be driving. Kathy, can you come with me?"

The three spent the next few minutes talking about how to handle the situation within the company. Marie would brief John when he came in and talk to him about how they would inform other team members, particularly Dean's engineering staff.

"Should you be driving?" Marie asked, wiping tears from her own eyes.

"Yeah, give me a few minutes," Scott said.

When Dean came out of Kathy's office, they exchanged hugs and a few words him.

Scott took the extra set of keys to Dean's Bronco off the company car key rack next to the receptionist desk and handed the keys to his own Sable to Kathy.

At Dean's home, they learned the details were horrible. Brenda had gone out for a late evening run around Purdue and West Lafayette. It was a safe community. Local police spend most of their time making sure that drunken students and residents got home safely at night. Now they had a killer to find. It appeared Brenda was grabbed, dragged into a parking structure, stripped, raped, stabbed and left for dead in freezing temperatures. She dragged herself 160 feet where a passerby found her in the morning.

Scott and Kathy stayed all morning until the number of Dean and Carol's family in the house made it clear they had plenty of support.

It wasn't a very productive week at Fairlane Tool, at least in the offices. Everybody read the details in the newspapers. The murder was the subject of every lunch conversation. The young design engineers did the best they could without Dean's guidance and deep understanding of the product, not wanting to call him under any circumstances. Even those few production workers who had never met Dean or any of the Williams family worried about their own children more.

The Williams family scheduled the funeral for the following Saturday morning. Dozens of Brenda's classmates made the 280-mile trek from Purdue. Perhaps 100 of her high school classmates were there, many coming a long way home from college to say their final goodbyes. Virtually all of Fairlane's management and office staff attended as well as some production workers who barely knew Dean and his family. Tears were shed, but most of all they asked, "Who would do such a thing?"

Chapter 37

Working for McGrath

Wednesday, February 27, 1991

John told Scott he wanted to talk with him about something important. Anderson anticipated a difficult discussion, but he never anticipated Scott would flat-out refuse when he asked him to work for McGrath.

"I'm sorry, John. I can't work for someone I don't respect. This guy, long ago, proved he's inept. Do the right thing. Get rid of him and run your own company."

"This is more complicated than you know," John said, looking at his hands.

"Well, will you let me in on it?" Scott said. "Are you dying or something? Is he blackmailing you? If I understood the problem, maybe I could help."

"I'm not sure what to do in this situation," John responded.

Scott raised his voice. "Well, I think that's pretty clear. Fire the asshole."

"That's what he said I should do with you," John said.

"On what grounds?"

"He says he can't get the information from accounting he needs to run the business," John responded.

"John, the guy is a devious tyrant. He has the best information system of any company our size. Everything he could possibly want could be at the tip of his fingers, yet he won't even try to learn how to access it. You can fire me, but I know you are going to fire him eventually. If you're still in business before you start to see clearly."

John started to say something. He opened his mouth as if he wanted to say something, and then shut it again. He and Scott just looked at each other for a minute. Both were tired; both were frustrated. Finally, Scott spoke.

"Look, I promised Mary I'd get home early tonight. Let's continue this discussion tomorrow."

"Yes, let's do that," John said softly.

Scott stood up and walked toward the door.

As they talked behind John's closed door anyone in the common area outside the door could see them talking. Since McGrath's office door faced the same open space, he could watch, but not hear, the conversation from his vantage point seated at his desk. As Scott left John's office, McGrath rose from his desk and met him in the hall.

"I'd like to see you in my office at 7:30 a.m.," McGrath said.

"Sorry," Scott said, "I don't get in until 8:30 and I have a meeting then," Scott responded, not breaking his stride as he brushed by McGrath who stood directly in his path to the stairway. He had a three-step head start when McGrath wheeled to follow him down the stairs.

"I said I wanted to talk to you at 7:30," McGrath said with a loud angry voice.

"And I said I wouldn't be there," Scott responded as McGrath followed him down the stairs.

This perceived insubordination made McGrath particularly angry. By now, Scott turned the corner, the bigger man well behind him. By the time McGrath cleared the landing Scott had put his hand on the fire door to the accounting offices.

"STOP!" he shouted. "I demand you look at me when you talk to me. That is no way to talk to your superior."

The remark stopped Scott in his tracks and McGrath stopped on the second from the bottom step as Scott turned toward him.

"You moron," Scott said to him with a tone of pity reserved for someone who has just done something unbelievably stupid. "You're not ANYBODY's superior. And looking at you frankly makes me sick to my stomach."

With those words, Scott pushed his way through the door to the accounting offices and McGrath followed him.

"Brave words, little man," McGrath said angrily, his face now flushed and bright pink.

"Is that the best you can come up with? Come on, you want to hit me. Why don't you do it? Your lawyer's kids need braces," Scott said in a firm voice loud enough for everyone else in the accounting bullpen to hear.

Debbie, Marie, Dave and Tom Hickey, the night supervisor, looked right at them as it happened. Perhaps the presence of four other people kept the confrontation from continuing. McGrath glared at Scott's back as he calmly walked into his office, turned off the light and locked the door, putting on his overcoat as he walked toward the front door. The clock said 5:05 p.m. as the front door shut. McGrath turned in the other direction, slamming the door at the north end of the accounting bullpen as he returned upstairs.

Those who remained said little. Tom and Marie quickly stopped talking about their human resources issue and he quickly vacated the area by heading down the south hallway away from McGrath. Marie went into her office and emerged with her coat on, turning out her office light as she pulled the door closed behind her. Debbie, too, pulled her coat from the closet by the front door and they exited together, perhaps in solidarity with Scott, perhaps seeking to leave the upsetting scene as soon as possible.

Dave made a more deliberate departure.

He carefully put away the papers on his desk and pushed the drawer shut on the fireproof file cabinet, pressing the key button into the "lock" position. Drinking the last gulp of his now cold coffee, he walked to the office break area and rinsed his cup. As he stood drying the cup with a paper towel, he saw John come down the stairs and pass through the fire door. Though Dave followed the same way a few seconds later, John seemed unaware of his presence.

Back in his office, Dave put on his suit jacket, then his overcoat, turned out his office light and closed the door. As he reached the front door, he flicked out all the lights in accounting except the single set above the door between the main first floor hallway and the lobby. He thought only McGrath remained in the office. Inserting his key into the door between the lobby and the atrium, he locked the front door behind him and walked out into the cold early evening. The time on his watch read 5:14 p.m. Looking up at the second floor, he saw the lava-light-like movement on a screen-saver in engineering. At the building's north end above the coffee room, he could see a light in McGrath's office and John's dark office across the hall.

"Wow!" Dave thought. "What did I just witness?" From his office, closest to the stairway, he had heard some of the loud argument through the door. It made him happy someone stood up to McGrath, but found it frightening his boss did it. High tension had become open warfare. He was proud of Scott but knew political battles rarely created anything but casualties. As he turned his car northward he thought; "Well, tonight I'm going to have a story to tell Lauren at dinner.

At home that night, Scott and Mary Mackenzie were glued to the television, like much of the rest of America, for an hour-long press conference by General Norman Schwarzkopf explaining Operation Desert Storm and the soon to be over Persian Gulf War.

Reporter: "Can I ask you two questions: First,...did you think it would be such an easy cakewalk as it seems and secondly, what are your impressions of Saddam Hussein as a military strategist?"

Schwartzkopf: "Ha! (Many others in the room laughed too.) Um, ah, first of all, if we thought it would be such an easy fight, we definitely wouldn't have stocked 60 days' worth of supplies in these log bases. So, as I told you all for a very, very long time, it is very, very important for a military commander never to assume away the capabilities of his enemy, and when you're facing an enemy that is over 500,000 strong, has a reputation that they've had of fighting for eight years, being combat hardened veterans, had the number of tanks and the type of equipment they've had, you don't assume away anything. So, we certainly didn't expect it to go this way. As far as Saddam Hussein being a great military strategist, he is neither a strategist nor is he schooled in the operational art, nor is he a tactician, nor is he a general, nor is he a soldier. Other than that, he is a great military man. I want you to know that." (Laughter from the press).

At the end of the news conference, Scott said, "Well, now maybe car sales will get back to something that resembles normal."

Chapter 38

Life's Too Short to Work for an Asshole

Thursday, February 28, 1991

Scott's busy schedule prevented him from talking to John in the morning. He and Kathy left for a late lunch together and did not return for almost two hours. Shortly after they returned, McGrath went into Kathy's office and closed the door.

"I talked to John Anderson this morning and you are going to start working for me starting immediately. Come up to my office at three-thirty." McGrath looked at the clock as he referred to the time, twenty minutes in the future. Kathy's eyes followed him, and then he walked out the door.

Fifteen seconds later, Kathy hurried to Scott's office and closed the door. Marie witnessed the whole exchange, as she stood behind the receptionist desk pretending to look at the incoming mail. She heard nothing McGrath said, but the situation worried her.

While Scott and Kathy talked, McGrath fumed in his office. Kathy did not arrive at three-thirty, or four or even four-thirty. At ten before five, they both walked past McGrath's office into John's office and closed the door. He could see them through the glass panel next to the door as they stood at John's desk. McGrath's face reddened at their insubordination. He could feel his blood pressure rise, but resolved to wait and talk to Anderson before he did anything. He could now see John standing, too, and he looked distressed. He didn't like how Scott seemed to be doing 80% of the talking.

Inside, John directed a question at Kathy. "Aren't you going to give us two weeks' notice?"

Scott responded for them both. "You're getting four weeks; you're just getting all four of them from me."

"Life's too short to work for an asshole," Kathy added.

The conversation continued for a few minutes and Kathy left John's office first. She walked into McGrath's open door, and casually tossed some keys on McGrath's desk. "I'm leaving so you'll need these for the computer room. Good luck with it." She left as quickly as she entered.

McGrath looked at the keys momentarily and rose from his desk. He saw Scott pass his door with a very happy, satisfied look on his face. That made him even angrier. He hurried to the door and hurled the first insult he could think of at the accountant: "So, when are you going to tell your wife you're fucking the help."

The comment stopped Mackenzie in his tracks. However, rather than catching him off guard, as McGrath hoped, the opportunity to answer the question seemed to please him.

"I can fully understand why you made that nasty remark. After knowing you for a year, it doesn't surprise me you would fuck your cousins. However, in my family we just don't do that." Scott knew McGrath would have no quick comeback. He smiled a broad smile, nodded at McGrath and disappeared down the remaining stairs.

McGrath turned and walked into John's office. "They're cousins?" he asked.

Downstairs, Kathy packed up as Marie and Debbie came into her office to find out what happened. The clock on

Kathy's wall now read 5:05 p.m. They knew little of the story when Scott walked in wearing his long grey wool coat. He gave Kathy a long hug. "I've got to scoot. I told Mike I'd help him with dress rehearsal tonight. Call me in the morning."

"Thanks, Cuz," she said as he walked out the door.

"Cuz?" Marie asked, turning towards Kathy. "You're cousins?" Kathy nodded. "You look nothing like each other!"

"His dad's Scotch, my dad's French. We can't help it," Kathy responded.

Soon Marie and Debbie knew the whole story. Scott hired his first cousin and wanted to avoid the appearance of nepotism. Only John, Dean and Michael knew about the relationship. At 5:40, the three women left together, each carrying boxes to Kathy's car.

Marie and Debbie helped Kathy brush heavy snow off her car. They each gave her a long hug. Marie then helped Debbie brush off her car and then turned her attention to her own. Marie turned the ignition key to warm up her minivan. Getting back out again, she extracted the long snowbrush from behind the driver's seat and swept away the sticky snow from her windows and headlights. Only one car remained in the parking lot as she turned her car southward.

At 6:05 p.m., Angus McGrath turned off the light in his second-floor office, tired and in a foul mood. He had an IT manager who had just walked out on him, an IT system he knew nothing about, and a CFO who had just given four weeks' notice. Anderson avoided talking to him. Would John change his mind? The CFO's influence helped get him fired at his last company. Maybe John would ask Scott to stay. This was not going well. He locked the door to his office, switched off the light in the second-floor reception area and then the light at the bottom of the stairway. Walking across the dimly lit accounting office, he took his overcoat from the closet across from the lobby door. He wrapped his scarf around his neck and deliberately buttoned up his jacket as he thought about the blowing snow he saw from his office window. Finally, he turned up his jacket collar as he went through the first of the three doors separating him from the parking lot, unlocking and then relocking the doors behind him.

Only two cars sat in the east parking lot. About three dozen remained in the south parking lot near the door where the manufacturing workers clocked in. Snow covered the white Mercury Sable in the third spot to the left of the front door. McGrath stopped at the side of the car and removed his gloves as he fumbled for car keys in his pocket. Behind him, he heard a CRACK sound as something seemed to bump his left shoulder. Then another CRACK and something bumped his other side. He did not hear the third CRACK of the bullet hitting him square in the back or the fourth CRACK penetrating the building next to where he lay face down in the snow.

No one heard the door slam on the car parked opposite his in the parking lot. The now heavy falling snow muffled every sound. If anyone stood there, they would only hear the dull sounds of the stamping presses through the closed bay doors. Thump, Thump, Thump, Thump, Thump....

Chapter 39

Dead in the Snow

A few minutes before 8 p.m., the guy who handled Fairlane's snow removal lowered the blade on his F-350 pickup truck where the south entrance met the side street. The heavy snowfall was almost over and only a light dusting continued to fall from the sky. At $200 per snowfall, plowing Fairlane's parking lot would be good money for an hour's work. The long, narrow, east parking lot would be easy work with only one car remaining as an obstacle to slow him down. He got out of the truck and angled the blade to the right so that he could make long fast passes that would throw the snow off the asphalt.

The first pass was along the east perimeter, throwing his work onto the snow covered grass strip between the parking lot and the street. Turning in the other direction, he threw snow toward the building, stopping short of the white Mercury that sat south of the front door. Backing up to take another run, the driver made a wide arc around the car and continued to the south end of the building. He didn't realize there was a dead man lying next to the Sable until he got out to shift the snowplow's angle. Blood was everywhere. Falling to his knees, he vomited. He didn't touch the man or even go near. He knew the man was dead and didn't want to look at his face. Stumbling to the south employee entrance, he found Bob Yost in the shipping area. Yost dashed to the supervisor's office where Tom Hickey immediately phoned Dearborn police. A squad car arrived in four minutes; a second squad car was there in six and an ambulance in seven. There was no need for the ambulance. Angus McGrath was obviously dead.

Tom's list of emergency phone contacts had not been updated since McGrath joined the company a year earlier. Jimmy's name was at the top of the list, but he was no longer with the company. Tom called Terry Delaney, who lived only about five miles from the plant. Delaney called John's home and Barbara said he was at a University of Michigan alumni event. Mary Mackenzie said that Scott was at a Players rehearsal. Delaney was able to talk to Ken Carpenter who got into his car to talk with police at the company.

By the time Delaney arrived, the EMS crew had transferred McGrath's body to the ambulance. Tom had already confirmed McGrath's identify, which the police already knew from the driver's license they found in his wallet. Ken would arrive fifteen minutes later.

There was little usable evidence in the parking lot. From the single hole in the building, the police surmised that McGrath had been shot with a small caliber weapon from a position directly east on the other side of the long, one aisle parking lot. The snowplow likely scraped away any shell casings.

Detective Ben Hassan began his questions with Tom. "Do you know of anyone who might want to kill this man?"

"That would be just about everyone in the company," Tom responded. He told Hassan about the argument between McGrath and Scott the previous night but he didn't think Scott was the kind of person who would kill McGrath.

Interviewing Terry, Hassan asked, "Do you know anything about an argument that Scott Mackenzie had with McGrath yesterday?"

"That would be news to me," Terry responded.

"Was there anyone else who had particular problems with Mr. McGrath lately?" Hassan asked.

"Jimmy Mack Jones, the former plant manager, but I don't think either of them would be the type to gun somebody down in the parking lot. It would be more likely one of the people in the plant. There are a lot of them that hated his guts."

"Did you hate his guts?" Hassan asked.

"I didn't like him, but I had no particular reason to kill him," Terry responded.

Hassan asked a few more questions and learned that Scott was supposed to be at The Players. Other officers interviewed the snowplow driver and learned that if they were to find any shell casings, they would likely be in the snow that the plow threw off the east side of the parking lot onto the grass and not in one of the larger piles at the end of the parking lot. Police taped off the east lot to prevent access in the morning and they allowed the driver to continue plowing the south parking lot where the hourly employees parked.

At a few minutes after 9:30 p.m., the phone rang at The Players. The old building only had three working phones plus a pay phone in the entry vestibule.

Roy Jendrzejewski answered the backstage phone and found Scott who was helping Michael clear the stage to make room for the night's last one-act rehearsal. "Mr. Mackenzie, this is Ben Hassan from the Dearborn police department. I'd like to ask you about an incident at the Fairlane Tool & Manufacturing Company. Could you tell me where you have been since 5 p.m.?"

Scott responded, "Well, I left the parking lot a few minutes after five, and drove to downtown Detroit. I got dinner at the Wendy's on Jefferson Avenue and then came over to the club."

"What time did you arrive at Wendy's?" Hassan asked.

"About 5:30," Scott responded.

"Can anyone verify your whereabouts this evening?" Hassan asked.

"Well," Scott continued, pulling out a scrap of paper from his pocket. "I've got the receipt in my hand that says I bought dinner at the Wendy's on Jefferson Avenue at 5:32 p.m. I arrived at the club less than five minutes after that. Michael Anderson, Bill Rohloff and Mike Mongan were standing in the lobby when I walked in the door. That should be pretty good proof of where I was. What is this all about anyway? Did something happen at the company?"

Through all of this questioning, Scott had given no indication that he knew of the crime that had been committed that evening, thus Hassan purposely gave him incomplete information. "A Mr. McGrath has been shot."

"In our offices?" Scott asked.

"No, in the parking lot."

"Is he dead?" Scott responded.

"Yes, he is," was Hassan's response.

"Well," said Scott, "I can see why you want to talk to me."

Forty minutes later, Scott and Michael showed up together at the Dearborn police department. Hassan talked to both of them separately and quickly got the sense that neither man was his killer. He received permission to look in Scott's car and found four bags of water softener salt, two snow scrapers, a copy of the Journal of Accountancy, two copies of Crain's Detroit Business, four days of the Wall Street Journal, a pair of old blue coveralls, safety flares and the kinds of things that people normally keep in their automobiles.

They tested Scott's hands and sleeves for gunshot residue, found none and let him go home. Now nearly midnight, this investigation wasn't going any further that night.

Chapter 40

Damage Control

Friday, March 1, 1991

Even in the Detroit metropolitan area where there are hundreds of homicides a year, news of an executive shot in his company's parking lot should generate significant media coverage. For news like this, it was very predictable that all three local TV stations would be on the scene doing in person interviews with seemingly anyone who was willing to stand in front of a camera. Somehow, McGrath's murder had failed to make the 11 o'clock news or the morning edition of the Detroit Free Press. However, by the time the day shift began at 7 a.m., two news crews were sitting in the south parking lot interviewing hourly workers as they got out of their cars and soon all three local TV stations were taking pictures of police officers looking for evidence in the east parking lot.

Finding the spent shell casings in a stamping company parking lot was not a welcome task for the two investigators who ran the metal detectors. Stamping company parking lots are notorious for collecting small metal slugs punched from the company's products. One detective knew how to adjust the metal detectors to search for brass and ignore steel from previous experience in a snowy parking lot. Two hours later, three of the four shell casings were in plastic evidence bags.

Knowing the press would want a statement in the morning, Scott and Michael called John at home after leaving the police station. They agreed to meet at a restaurant near the plant at 7 a.m. to work up a statement for the press. The next morning, the three of them plus Ken, Terry and the company's lawyer were sitting with breakfast and several yellow legal pads in front of them. The lawyer had hired a security firm who would restrict outsider access to company property and potentially search employees who went into the building. They agreed that John would make the statement, which the lawyer and Scott primarily crafted.

"Last night, Angus "Bull" McGrath was shot and killed in our company's parking lot. Our condolences go out to his widow and three children. While he had spent only a year with our company, he had a distinguished career in the automotive parts manufacturing industry. Dearborn police have interviewed many of our personnel already but have given us no indication that any of those interviewed is a suspect at this time. We have hired a security firm to protect our worker's safety until this case is solved and further questions about this case should be directed to Dearborn police."

All day on Friday, Dearborn police camped out in Fairlane's offices. Having decided that he could trust Scott Mackenzie, detective Hassan decided he could use a CPA's investigative skills and paired Scott with one of his junior officers to go through McGrath's files to try to find anything that might give the investigation some direction. When Scott pointed out that Dave Johnson had similar experience, Hassan interviewed Dave and decided that he had neither the motive nor personality of a killer and that he would be useful in coordinating employee interviews.

Scott and Dave's involvement lasted until well after lunchtime.

Late in the afternoon, John walked into Scott's office and sat down in the guest seat beside his desk. "I was wondering if maybe you'd stay now. Perhaps Kathy would come back, too."

Scott looked at John long and hard. He reached out for his half-empty cup and filled his mouth with room temperature coffee. He swallowed, took another sip, and then set the cup down on the moisture-stained leather coaster on his desk.

"That ship sailed a long time ago. I started looking for a new job the day after you made your lunch buddy speech. I interviewed with a couple of other companies, but I really wanted to start my own. Kathy, Mark and I came up with an idea over dinner one night and we've been working on writing software for three months. We'll be ready to demonstrate to customers in a couple of weeks. We're gone.

"I suggest you get down on your knees and beg Jimmy and Denise to come back, maybe give him his stock back as a signing bonus. McGrath did a lot of damage to this company; now you're going to have to rebuild it without me."

And that was it. John lost his COO, CFO and IT Manager in a matter of hours. Thinking about his situation overnight, he walked into Dave Johnson's office the next morning, promoted him to Controller and gave him a 40% raise. Then he invited Marie to his office for a long discussion about how they would replace the talent they had lost. He was sure it would take some time, but was not sure he had the will power to do it.

Chapter 41

The Aftermath

Two Years Later - Wednesday, February 3, 1993

Scott and Mary Mackenzie enjoyed a quiet moment in their dining room after dinner. Scott, a beer drinker by nature, had a half inch of wine left in his glass and Mary a little less. Their children were playing with blocks, puzzles and a computer game in the family room. When the phone rang, Scott rose and answered the call on the kitchen wall phone. He recognized the voice instantly.

"Dave Johnson, you're a blast from the past! What's going on?"

Scott quickly learned that John was planning to sell the company. While Dave was one of the few people who knew what was going on, he thought he should brush up his résumé and wanted advice on the wording and permission to use Scott as a reference. They agreed to meet for lunch on a Saturday, a week and a half away. Dave added, "I have a lot to catch you up on."

"Anything big?" Scott asked.

"Well, did you hear they caught the guy who murdered Brenda Williams?"

"No, tell me about it."

"Apparently a local guy was trying to break into a woman's apartment in another town, just up the road. She called police and they caught the guy. Upon questioning, he confessed to murdering Brenda and a woman from Indianapolis as well. The trial was quick and he got two life sentences."

Dave gave him a few more details, including an update on how Dean and Carol were weathering the trauma. Then Scott asked, "How about the other murder?" Dave surprised him by asking, "Which one?"

"You've had more than one?"

"Well, sort of. The police never figured out who killed McGrath, but in the meantime, Stacy D'Angelo was arrested for killing her husband, Tony. It happened just a few weeks after you left."

"I never saw anything about it," Scott replied.

"It wasn't exactly front page news. I never saw it in the Free Press. Marie found out about it in one of the downriver newspapers. Apparently, Stacy and Tony had a fight in the kitchen. She said he tried to hit her, and she tried to defend herself with a chef's knife. Then she went into the bedroom and locked the door. She said she thought she just nicked him but came out in the morning and found him dead in a pool of blood on the kitchen floor from a knife wound to the neck. They both had cocaine in their systems so the prosecutor let her plead guilty to possession of a controlled substance. She'll probably be out in a few months."

Scott and Dave agreed that they had a lot to talk about and agreed to cover the rest in person. When he hung up the phone, he gave Mary the complete update, ending by saying, "You know, I haven't talked to Mike in almost two years either. I think I'll call him too."

Mary suggested, "You've only been to Players once in the last couple of years. Frolic Saturday would be this weekend. Why don't you two go to the Pre-Frolic dinner and catch up with him there?"

Scott called Michael Anderson a few minutes later and made plans to meet.

Chapter 42

The Reunion

Saturday, February 6, 1993

Turning left off Mack Avenue; Michael Anderson parked on Beaconsfield, the small side street next to Tom's Oyster Bar in Gross Pointe Park. He left the car running as the parking valet trotted across the street and handed him a numbered ticket. Stepping inside, a dozen tuxedoed men stood at the bar; making it a tight squeeze to the restaurant's back dining areas. "The Players are to the left, all the way in the backroom," the hostess said, seeing Michael's tuxedo under his camel overcoat.

Shaking a few hands as he passed Players at the bar, Michael proceeded towards the "backroom." The room sat furthest from the corner of the three storefronts the Oyster Bar occupied and was not actually at the "back" of the restaurant. He inserted his gloves into his overcoat's two front pockets and hung it among many others on hooks just inside the backroom door. He turned to see a pretty blonde server waiting for his drink order. Standing nearly a foot taller than she, he liked the way her blue eyes met his as he placed an order for the restaurant's signature Oyster Ale.

Michael surveyed gentlemen enjoying drinks before the Pre-Frolic Dinner. Recognizing his old coworker nearby from the back of his red head he called, "Scott Mackenzie! How are you?"

"Mike! It seems like forever. What has it been, two years?"

The restaurant pushed groups of two and four person tables together to make three long tables for ten each. Scott and Michael took two of the last three seats, sitting across from each other with an empty seat at the end.

"Catch me up," Michael said. "How are you and Kathy doing with RealView?"

"Great!" Scott said. "I'll tell you all about us, but then you have to tell me about Fairlane. I haven't talked to anybody there for over a year."

Mike nodded his agreement and Scott continued. "Kathy finished getting demonstration software together within a few weeks after I left Fairlane. Mark demonstrated it to a bunch of the real estate franchises in the Detroit area and got six offices in the Northwest suburbs to test an alpha version almost immediately.

"Initially we thought we would download home pictures using a phone line connection to each real estate office. Each night our computer would dial the computer in each office, download the new listings since the previous day, and delete the old ones. Keeping the right pictures on every computer challenged us. If something interrupted a transmission, an office might end up having old pictures our software would never delete or miss new listings. Picture resolution required experimentation. Initially, we made the resolution higher than we needed, which made the file transfer time too long. Fortunately, we learned quickly. It took about three months to get all the parts working the way we wanted."

"OK, enough with the technical stuff", Michael said. "The big picture, how is your business doing?"

"Well enough, I think. We employ about 20 programmers now and are in about ten metropolitan markets. Right now, we're working on converting our software to make the nightly downloads happen using the internet. Our transfer speeds are not very good right now, but modems get faster all the time and we anticipate in a few years we'll store all of the images on our server and we can skip the downloads. A real estate agent could just access our website and look at pictures of any house they want."

"I've been thinking of getting Prodigy or Compuserve," Michael said. "I don't quite understand how the internet works. Could someone access your service through Prodigy?"

"If they had a RealView subscription," Scott said.

"We've actually got another software company looking to buy us. They're talking in terms of paying $8 million for our technology. It seems like an awful lot of money for two years work, but who am I to argue?"

"How much of the company is yours?" Michael inquired.

"I initially put in the same amount of money as Kathy and Mark so at first they owned half and I owned half. We gave equity to some of our programmers, so now we each own about 45%. If we sold out, I would probably go on and do something else, Mark would go with the new owners and Kathy would stay home with the kids."

"They have kids?" Mike asked.

"Yeah, Kathy got pregnant just before we started the company but she didn't know it yet. Now they've got another one on the way. Anyhow, for $3.4 million, I wouldn't really need to work again, but I would."

"3.4 million? Scott, that's fabulous!"

"Yeah, it beats chasing down inventory errors at a manufacturing company. What's going on at Fairlane?" Scott asked.

"Chaos," Michael replied, "mostly chaos." He paused as the blonde server brought his Oyster Ale and asked if Scott would like another drink.

"Yes, I'll have the same thing," he replied.

"Are you guys performing tonight?" she asked. Scott shook his head "no", but Michael told her about his role as an Air Force officer in a Player-written show. She loved acting. This job paid for her drama major at Wayne State University. Michael's blue eyes met her blue eyes as she described her aspirations for professional theater after graduating in a few months. Drink orders from farther down the table interrupted her and Scott and Michael went back to talking shop.

"Anyhow, you wouldn't believe how chaotic the last two years have been. John brought in some twit as CFO. Anytime anybody needed any financial information he kept saying he'd have to ask Dave. He never seemed to do any work himself. So finally, John just fired him and promoted Dave to CFO. Dave hired a new assistant Controller who seems to be working out pretty well."

"So who's running operations?" Scott asked.

"Ken is, at least he's doing his best. John doesn't seem to have his heart in this business anymore, so I suspect he's selling the company. A group of guys in suits toured the place a few weeks ago with no explanation so I'm guessing they're buyers."

The blonde server brought back Scott's drink. While he was pulling out a five-dollar bill, she slipped Michael a folded cocktail napkin. "If you're interested," she said.

"Thank-you" he replied, unfolding the napkin so that he could read what was written on it. "I believe I am." Obviously pleased with herself, the blonde turned away from the table without noticing Scott holding his money out to her.

"April Loggins," Michael said as he put the cocktail napkin in his jacket pocket.

"Just once I'd like that to happen to me," Scott responded.

"You've done alright for yourself, my friend," Michael said. "You have a beautiful wife and two beautiful kids. Women throwing themselves at you is both a blessing and a curse. Yeah, meeting women has always been easy for me, but look what I've got for it, a wrecked marriage because I was weak too many times when temptation presented itself. I'd rather be in your shoes, really."

"OK" Scott said. "I can appreciate what you're saying, but it would have been fun to experience your predicament for a few years. By the way, it's three kids now. We had a boy fourteen months ago."

The two servers handling the room divided the tables between them. An older server now took the food orders for their table. Distracted and unprepared to order, both Scott and Michael hastily ordered the same salmon as the Player sitting next to them.

The conversation returned to Scott's children. They consumed the salad and most of the entrée before they talked about Fairlane again.

"Did the police ever get a theory as to who shot McGrath?" Scott asked.

"Hell, Scott, even I don't have a theory about who shot the guy and I think about it almost every day. Granted, everybody hated him, but if somebody shot every asshole executive, there wouldn't be an intact management team in any decent-sized company in the United States. Frankly, I don't think anybody there hated him bad enough to kill him." With three bullets in him, it looked more like a crime of passion. You know, like what an ex-girlfriend would do if she was really pissed off at you."

"I don't have any direct experience with that," Scott responded.

"Everything still seems bizarre. I never knew a murder victim before, and then Brenda Williams, McGrath and Tony D'Angelo all die within a few weeks. It scared me to go outside for a while."

"I heard about Tony," Scott replied. Kathy reconnected with Marie a few days ago and they caught up. Marie said there's a good chance Stacy will receive parole in a couple of weeks."

"That's news to me, Scott. I've been so busy; I'm not up on all the company scuttlebutt. Then again, I probably haven't talked to Marie in a couple of weeks either even though I must past her office a minimum of four times a day."

The catching up conversation went quickly and easily. Fellow Player, Tom Brandel, the restaurant's owner, sent a round of cognac to the 30 Players. Scott and Michael took polite sips as someone toasted their host, but neither particularly liked cognac and they needed to be sober to drive themselves to the club.

Snow fell as they emerged from The Oyster Bar and there was already a half inch of snow on the ground. The light wind and 12°F temperature combined to make it downright uncomfortable to stand outside while the two valets retrieved cars for the thirty tuxedoed men who almost simultaneously emerged from the restaurant.

One valet pulled Scott's green Mercury Sable right behind Michael's white Sable and Scott followed Michael to the Berke Medical Clinic's fenced in parking lot next to the club. The off-duty police officers hired for security directed them to park along the back fence the Playhouse shared with the clinic.

Scott's glasses frosted over as he entered the club's warm interior. As he wiped the lenses with his handkerchief, club patriarch Bill Rohloff greeted them as they stepped into the lobby. As usual, Rohloff called them by both names, "Hello Michael Anderson, Hello Scott Mackenzie. Long time, no see, Scott. How have you been?" Since Michael needed to get in costume for the second one-act, he cut the conversation short and excused himself.

Scott volunteered to hang up Michael's coat and Scott spent a few minutes catching up with Rohloff before climbing the wide spiral staircase to hang the coats in the hallway adjoining the theater's balcony. He hung Michael's camel hair coat on one of the metal hooks placed well above Scott's own eye level. He looked at Michael's coat as he first removed his scarf, then his grey wool overcoat and hung it on the adjacent hook. He chuckled to himself as he recalled how mad McGrath became when Michael went home with his keys.

Walking into the Founders Room, Scott noted the addition of several Players beer mugs with black ribbons memorializing members who had died, high on the wall above the former president's portraits. Scott poked around the "M-N-O" shelf to find his beer mug, finding himself behind Mike Mongan.

Standing behind the bar working the beer tap were Chuck Steltencamp, a Troy High School English teacher, and Roy Jendrzejewski. Steltencamp described the beer choices as dark, red and pilsner and Scott asked him to fill his mug with the red. He shook a few hands as he went from the lobby into the theater itself and briefly stood in the door to survey the room.

An idea now distracted him. Four of the six front row tables were full including Scott's usual house left aisle table. Though many familiar faces stood in the lobby, Scott uncharacteristically sat alone on the left side of the auditorium near the back. He did not really listen to the Player's Chorus performing Broadway show tunes to warm up the audience or pay much attention to the first two shows including the one featuring Michael.

At a few minutes before 10:30 p.m., Michael slipped into the chair next to Scott with his own beer mug just as the curtain rose for the evening's third one-act play. Two other second show cast members were with him. All Scott was able to say was "nice job" before the dialog began on stage. The evening's third show, **So When You Get Married**, the story of a half Italian/half Jewish single woman whose Italian mother and grandmother want her to marry and have children was easily the best production.

As the curtain came down on the third show, Michael got them both a beer refill while Scott distributed the plates, napkins and silverware stacked on the table. The Frolic Supper, the night's second meal, featured much simpler fare than at the Oyster Bar. Members with white butcher's coats over their tuxedo shirts served platters of bratwurst, sauerkraut, dinner rolls with butter and sugar cookies.

"An all-white meal like this would amuse my mother," Scott said. "She believes a plate should contain a variety of colors."

"Well, at least the condiments provide some contrast," said Michael, passing around the mustard. Scott cut the bratwurst with his knife and fork, dipping the medallions in the mustard and occasionally taking a sip of beer to wash it down.

The afterglow, featuring a series of sketches under the theme **Everything You Wanted to Know about Sex**, was awful; driving Michael's other cast members to the lobby.

When the afterglow was over, Scott started the conversation right away. "I've been thinking about the McGrath thing. I need to ask you a potentially embarrassing question and it's important for you to give me a straight, honest answer. Will you do that?"

"That sounds like the kind of question my doctor asks me when he wants to know my sexual history," Michael half-joked.

"I'm dead serious," Scott responded.

"Come-on Scott," Michael said. "I'll give you the straight scoop unless it's something which is none of your business, in which case I'll tell you it's none of your business."

"OK, then, did you ever make anyone mad enough to want to kill you?"

"No," Michael shot back quickly, without reflecting on his response.

"Earlier this evening you made a remark about what an ex-girlfriend might do if she was really pissed off at you. How many of those women are lurking in your past?" Scott asked.

"Not more than one or two. You know, like the *Eagles* song."

"The Eagles song?" Scott asked

"You know, '*Four that want to own me, two that want to stone me, one said she's a friend of mine*'...," Michael replied.

"Right, **Take is Easy**," Scott said. "In my fantasy the girl's got long blonde hair, faded blue jeans, a blue denim work shirt, cowboy hat, no make-up and it's a red Ford stake truck, not a flatbed."

"The song doesn't say she's a blonde," Michael protested.

"Like I said, it's my fantasy," Scott replied. "Anyhow, let's talk about the two who want to stone you. Was one of these women particularly mad at you two years ago?" Scott asked the question with no levity in his voice, causing Michael to become suddenly serious too.

"Where are you going with this?" Michael asked.

"Well, upstairs you have a coat that looks just like the one McGrath wore when somebody shot him. As I recall, I helped you unload props from his Explorer that night which must have meant he was driving your car. Isn't it possible an angry girlfriend shot the wrong guy?"

The color in Michael's face seemed to disappear suddenly. "Oh, my god!" he said. He looked at Scott and Scott looked at him. Michael's face drew taut as he stared at the empty space over Scott's right shoulder. Scott looked intently at his face but waited patiently for Michael to think over the situation. The silence lasted almost a minute, near the end of which Michael's head gently began to nod.

"You know who did it," Michael said.

"I do?" Scott responded.

"She never could see without her glasses!"

Scott hadn't known who did it, but when Michael mentioned not wearing glasses, one name immediately came to mind. "Stacy D'Angelo? You got involved with Stacy D'Angelo?"

"Look, she came on to me. I didn't instigate it. It started right after she got her promotion and then after she got fired, we would still meet sometimes on Fridays. I thought she was just looking for a little adventure, then when she said she was planning to leave Tony, things started to get way too serious and I broke it off. She'd call me and I finally just stopped taking her calls."

"How does the timing compare to when McGrath was shot?" Scott asked.

"I think the last time I actually talked to her on the phone was a little before Valentine's Day, so McGrath got shot about two weeks later."

"Where would she get a gun?"

"Tony had lots of guns," Michael noted. "She mentioned it to me on several occasions. She said he was the jealous type and he would kill her if he ever found out she was sleeping with me."

"Well, maybe he found out and tried to kill you instead," Scott speculated. "Either way, both of them had a motive."

Even with the playhouse clearing out there were too many people around for this to be a good place to talk. A little while later, they were at the IHOP restaurant southwest on Jefferson Avenue, each with a mug of coffee in front of them.

"Mike, you've got to talk to the police about this. You don't know if it was Tony or Stacy. If it was Stacy, while it's possible jail time has mellowed her, there is also the distinct possibility it has made her even more pissed off at you."

"Yeah," Michael said with regret in his voice. "I'll do that."

Chapter 43

Cold Case

Michael met detective Hassan at the Dearborn police station first thing Monday morning. Michael nervously sipped his coffee as Hassan located a yellow legal pad from his side desk drawer. "Tell me your theory," Hassan said, looking at Michael intently, as he attempted to judge the credibility of this tall, good-looking young man. Michael's theory made sense to Hassan who expressed his gratitude and promised to investigate this new lead on the two-year old case.

McGrath died in Dearborn and Stacy killed Tony in Southgate. With this new information, the two police departments began to collaborate. The Dearborn police compared the fingerprints recovered from a shell casing from the McGrath crime scene with those the Southgate police took from Tony D'Angelo's body. They matched, establishing a gun Tony loaded shot McGrath. However, it did not necessarily establish Tony fired the gun. Dearborn Police never found the .32 caliber handgun that shot McGrath. Southgate police did not find a .32 handgun either, although they found several other loaded unregistered handguns in Tony's gun safe, as well as an inventory of .32 caliber ammunition without a corresponding weapon. These facts were of no particular significance to the investigating officers when Stacy killed Tony with a knife since his death did not involve a gun. No one drew a connection to McGrath's murder. After all, neither Stacy nor Tony ever met Angus McGrath.

When questioned, Stacy said she suspected Tony might have killed McGrath in a case of mistaken identity, thinking it was Michael. This did not explain why she did not attempt to warn Michael after McGrath's murder or why she didn't come forward with this information during the original investigation. Forensic analysis showed that one of Stacy's winter coats had gunshot residue on it, which she explained by saying that Tony sometimes took her for target practice. The owner of a local indoor shooting range verified this statement.

"An attractive brunette who knows her way around firearms is not easy to forget," the range owner said.

Two years in jail made Stacy a difficult person to pressure in an interrogation room and the female assistant district attorney assigned to the case was sympathetic to her story. Dearborn police concluded either Tony or Stacy D'Angelo killed Angus McGrath. While the prosecutor never charged Stacy in McGrath's murder, the fact she withheld evidence after-the-fact delayed her parole on the drug charge another 18 months.

Michael left the Detroit Metro Area just in case Stacy blamed him for her 38 months in prison. He took a job selling sailboats in Naples, Florida only a few days after his brother announced he was selling Fairlane to a Minneapolis investment group that was doing a "roll-up" of smaller automotive suppliers. In Naples, Michael met a woman at the yacht club who had a successful medical practice and loved boats. He married her within a year.

A month after leaving prison, Stacy moved to Las Vegas to start a new life as a bartender. Marie learned about Stacy's move when she called the company to inquire about her 401(k) account. Marie passed the information to John who immediately told his brother. Michael slept much better knowing Stacy lived 2,500 miles away.

Stacy thought the gambling Mecca was the right place for her and felt very lucky despite having spent more than 3 years in prison. After all, not many people get away with murder twice.

If you enjoyed *Tool and Die*, please post a review with one or more of the on-line booksellers.